ESSAYS ON

LITERATURE & SOCIETY

*

Enlarged and Revised Edition

By the same Author

*

Essays

TRANSITION

THE STRUCTURE OF THE NOVEL

THE ESTATE OF POETRY

SCOTT AND SCOTLAND

Poems

FIRST POEMS

CHORUS OF THE NEWLY DEAD

THE MARIONETTE
(A Novel)

AN AUTOBIOGRAPHY

ESSAYS ON
LITERATURE
AND
SOCIETY

By
EDWIN MUIR

*Enlarged and Revised
Edition*

HARVARD UNIVERSITY PRESS
CAMBRIDGE, MASSACHUSETTS
1967

First published 1949
This Enlarged and Revised Edition
First published 1965
Reprinted 1967

Contents

ESSAYS ON LITERATURE AND SOCIETY

III

ROBERT HENRYSON

ENRYSON'S poetry has two main virtues; one the property of his age, the other more specifically his own. The first is as important as the second. He lived near the end of a great age of settlement, religious, intellectual and social; an agreement had been reached regarding the nature and meaning of human life, and the imagination could attain harmony and tranquillity. It was one of those ages when everything, in spite of the practical disorder of life, seems to have its place; the ranks and occupations of men; the hierarchy of animals; good and evil; the earth, heaven and hell; and the life of man and of the beasts turns naturally into a story because it is part of a greater story about which there is general consent. Henryson, like Chaucer, exists in that long calm of storytelling which ended with the Renaissance, when the agreement about the great story was broken. There is still an echo of the tranquillity in Spenser. But in *The Faerie Queene* he deals with the delightful creatures of his fancy, and Chaucer and Henryson deal with men and women, wolves and sheep, cats and mice.

The virtue of the story while it lasted was that it made everything natural, even tragedy; so that while pity had a place, there was no place for those outcries against life which fill the tragic drama of the next age. The framework and the nature of the story excluded them. And the pity itself is different from that of the Elizabethans, as deep, but tranquillised by the knowledge that tragedy has its place in the story. The poet accepts life, as the Eliza-

bethans tried to do, but is also resigned to it; the acceptance implying the resignation, and the resignation the
acceptance. This attitude makes the age between Chaucer
and Henryson the great age of the story. The Elizabethan
drama arose when the long peace of storytelling was
broken.

The sense that all life, whether of the animals or of men,
is a story and part of a greater story, is then one of the
surviving virtues of Henryson's poetry, strong enough
still, in spite of all that has happened since, to produce a
composing effect on us and remind us of a standard of
proportion which has been lost. It is the virtue of an age,
not ours, and it required to embody it a particular form
of art, not ours, and in the practice of that art Henryson
was almost perfect.

> Upon ane tyme (as Esope culd Report)
> Ane lytill Mous came till ane Revir syde;
> Scho micht not waid, hir schankis were sa schort,
> Scho culd not swym, scho had na hors to ryde:
> Of verray force behovit hir to byde,
> And to and fra besyde that Revir deip
> Scho ran, cryand with mony pietuous peip.

We recognise the narrative art of an age, which passed
with that age. In Henryson what delights us is the perfection with which it is controlled, its speed, which is neither
hurried nor lumbering, and the momentary touches of
humour and fancy which, while never retarding the story,
give it interest and vivacity:

> Scho culd not swym, scho had na hors to ryde.

Henryson's personal contribution to that consummate
art was a fanciful eye for detail and a profound sense of
situation, most usually comic, but in one or two cases
tragic. *The Moral Fabillis of Esope the Phrygian* is his great
humorous, and *The Testament of Cresseid* his great tragic

work. During the last century *The Fables* have been over-shadowed by *The Testament,* and their beauties neglected. But to appreciate the sweetness and harmony, the endlessly lively and inventive quality of Henryson's poetry, it is necessary to know them both; otherwise he runs the danger of being considered a poet of moderate capacity who, by a piece of good luck, wrote one great poem.

Most of the fables, though not all, are humorous. Henryson's humour is not quite like anything else in Scottish literature, more subtle and pervasive than the humour of Dunbar or Burns or Scott, more urbane, more indirect, less specialised, and saturated with irony. It is an assumption more than anything else; it remains implicit in the selection of detail and the choice of expression, and rarely comes to the point of statement. The fables transport us into a mood in which we see everything as Henryson sees it, with the same tender ironical humour, but without being able to explain very clearly how the mood has been induced. His sense of the ridiculous is so delicate and exact that the faintest emphasis is sufficient to indicate it, and more than the faintest would distort it. His more obvious strokes of humour, therefore, do not represent him best; as, for instance, when the fox kills a young lamb at Lent, dips it in the stream, and fishes it out, crying:

'*Ga doun schir Kid, cum up schir salmond agane.*'

The quality which transmutes these fables and our mood as we read them is less obvious and more delicate, and consists in a fine decorative sense of the absurd. We find it in the account of the Burgess Mouse on her way to visit her sister in the country:

Bairfute, allone, with pykestaf in hir hand,
As pure pylgrime scho passit out of town,
To seik hir sister baith oure daill and down.

We find it in the lament of Pertok the hen for Chanteclere
carried off by the fox:

> '*Allace*,' quod Pertok, makand sair murning,
> With teiris grit attour hir cheikis fell;
> '*Yone wes our drowrie, and our dayis darling*,
> Our nichtingall, and als our Orloge bell,
> Our walkryfe watche, us for to warn and tell
> Quhen that Aurora with hir curcheis gray
> Put up hir heid betwix the nicht and day.

> '*Quha sall our lemman be? quha sall us leid?*
> Quhen we ar sad, quha sall unto us sing?
> With his sweit Bill he wald brek us the breid.
> In all this warld wes thair ane kynder thing?
> In paramouris he wald do us plesing,
> At his power, as nature did him geif.
> Now eftir him, allace, how sall we leif?'

In this passage Henryson's sense of the ridiculous is
touched with pity, as it often is, and the pity with fantasy.
The pity is real, but as we feel it we smile at it, yet without
thinking the less of it. The touches in these verses are
exquisite:

> Our nichtingall, and als our Orloge bell, . . .
> With his sweit Bill he wald brek us the breid. . . .
> In all this warld wes thair ane kynder thing? . . .

These felicitous inventions run through *The Fables* and
give the dry stories their delightful life. They stray even
into the Moralitas with which each fable ends. These little
sermons have been blamed for their dullness, but one
suspects that in many of them Henryson retains his irony.
It is difficult to believe that a man with such a fine sense
of the ridiculous could have written without knowing what
he was doing,

> *The hennis are warkis that ffra ferme faith proceidis,*

at the end of a fable where hens and various beasts play their part. And the more serious of the Moralitas have a sincerity that is far from dullness.

The allegory is a form which the modern taste finds stilted and unreal, because the great story as Chaucer and Henryson knew it is dead. But while that story lasted the allegory was a perfectly natural convention—the most convenient device for telling it. *The Fables* belong to that modest kind of allegory which finds in the lives of the animals a pattern of human life. It has obvious merits; it simplifies life; it so reduces the dimensions of the human situation that we can easily grasp them; it divests the characters of all adventitious pomp and glory, as well as of all that passes in our time under the name of ideology; it lays bare with a force beyond the reach of literary naturalism the solid egoistic motives of action. This is doubtless what once made it such a popular and democratic form of art.

But in Henryson it assumes virtues of a rarer kind. Human snobbishness becomes touching and forgivable to him when he finds it in the Burgess Mouse. The crimes of the Fox and the Wolf become imaginatively comprehensible, and to that extent excusable, since all the animals act in accordance with their nature. The result is that the animal allegory, when it is not employed satirically, runs the danger of making us indiscriminately indulgent to all the faults and crimes of mankind; and the more lively the imagination of the poet, the more completely he enters into the nature of his allegorical characters, the Lion, the Wolf, the Fox, the Cat, the greater this danger becomes. So the fable has to be followed by the Moralitas, that human proportion may be preserved.

There are one or two fables in which Henryson achieves a profound effect of tragedy and pity, and moves us quite differently. An instance is *The Preiching of the Swallow*. It is distinguished from the other fables by the solemnity of the opening:

> The hie prudence, and warking mervelous,
> The profound wit of God omnipotent,
> Is sa perfyte, and sa Ingenious,
> Excellend ffar all mannis Jugement;
> For quhy to him all thing is ay present,
> Rycht as it is, or ony tyme sall be,
> Befoir the sicht off his Divinitie.

The argument proceeds in this vein to the conclusion

> That God in all his werkis wittie is.

The seasons are advanced in illustration of this, and Henryson describes how he walked out on a spring day to watch the labourers in the fields; and thereupon he suddenly comes upon the tragic theme of the poem. A flock of birds alights on a hedge near by; they are having a loud dispute with a Swallow, who has been warning them of their danger.

> 'Schir Swallow' (quod the Lark agane) and leuch,
> 'Quhat haif ye sene that causis yow to dreid?'
> 'Se ye yone Churll' (quod scho) 'beyond yone pleuch,
> Fast sawand hemp, and gude linget seid?
> Yone lint will grow in lytill tyme in deid,
> And thairoff will yone Churll his Nettis mak,
> Under the quhilk he thinkis us to tak.
>
> 'Thairfoir I rede we pas quhen he is gone,
> At evin, and with our naillis scharp and small
> Out off the eirth scraip we yone seid anone,
> And eit it up; ffor, giff it growis, we sall
> Haif caus to weip heirefter ane and all.'

In June Henryson walks out again

> Unto the hedge under the Hawthorne grene

and the birds come and resume their dispute. The Swallow
cries:

> '*O, blind birdis! and full of negligence,*
> *Unmyndful of your awin prosperitie,*
> *Lift up your sicht, and tak gude advertence;*
> *Luke to the Lint that growis on yone le;*
> *Yone is the thing I bad forsuith that we,*
> *Quhill it wes seid, suld rute furth off the eird;*
> *Now is it Lint, now is it hie on breird.*
>
> '*Go yit, quhill it is tender and small,*
> *And pull it up, let it na mair Incres;*
> *My flesche growis, my bodie quaikis all,*
> *Thinkand on it I may not sleep in peis. . . .*
>
> '*The awner off yone lint ane fouler is,*
> *Richt cautelous and full off subteltie;*
> *His pray full sendill tymis will he mis,*
> *Bot giff we birdis all the warrer be;*
> *Full mony off our kin he hes gart de,*
> *And thocht it bot ane sport to spill thair blude;*
> *God keip me ffra him, and the halie Rude.*'

The lint ripens and is gathered and spun into thread,
and the net is woven for the fowler's use. Winter comes;
the fowler clears a place in the snow and strews chaff on it
to attract the birds, and while they scrape and scratch he
throws the net over them.

> *Allace! it was grit hart sair for to se*
> *That bludie Bowcheour beit thay birdis doun,*
> *And ffor till heir, quhen thay wist weill to de,*
> *Thair cairfull sang and lamentatioun;*
> *Sum with ane staf he straik to eirth on swoun:*
> *Off sum the heid he straik, off sum he brak the crag,*
> *Sum half on lyve he stoppit in his bag.*

The poem produces a strong feeling of approaching danger and of a blindness that no warning can pierce. It is

filled with pity and a sort of second-sight which makes one think of Cassandra:

> '*This grit perrell I tauld thame mair than thryis;*
> *Now ar thay deid, and wo is me thairfoir!*'

There is an echo of the last line in *The Testament of Cresseid*.

The continuous interest and liveliness of the detail makes *The Fables* one of the most delightful books in Scottish literature. Detail is a matter of invention, an imaginative conclusion from the facts given; it creates the body of the story, which otherwise would be a mere bare framework. Situation is an imaginative conclusion on a greater scale, and gathers up a larger number and variety of elements. Henryson's genius is shown in his invention in both kinds, and *The Testament of Cresseid* is his great achievement in situation. It seems to have been his own invention purely; Mr. Harvey Wood in his consummate edition of Henryson implies it, and Sir Herbert Grierson is of the same opinion. 'It was no light thing', he says, 'to come after Boccaccio and to succeed in making a real addition to a great dramatic story, something that without needless challenging of comparison does, in its impressive way, complete that tragic tale.'

In his essay Sir Herbert speculates on the reason why Henryson should have been moved to add to a tale already accepted, and in the course of doing so he says the best things that have yet been said about the poem. 'Chaucer had, in his courtly and detached manner, avoided any moral judgment upon Cresseid. . . . The only moral which he will enforce at the end of the whole tale is the religious one—that all earthly things are vanity. . . . But Henryson is not content with what, after all, is an evasion—he, a Scot and a Schoolemaister, with a Scot's and a schoolmaster's belief in retribution. The result

might have been disastrous—a dry or a piously unreal
didactic poem. But it is not, and that for two reasons. In
the first place, Henryson retains Chaucer's sympathy with
Cresseid. . . . In the second place, his morality is sound
and sincere, not the preacher's conventional acceptance
of standards which he has not made his own. For the
retribution which overtakes Cresseid in the poem is the
retribution of her own heart. . . . It is not the leprosy we
think of as her penalty but the last encounter with Troilus
and its reaction on her own soul.' And Sir Herbert goes
on to say that when the poem ends it has produced 'a real
catharsis leaving us at peace with Cresseid as Chaucer's
poem scarcely does'.

There is only one thing in this criticism with which one
is tempted to disagree. I mean the assumption that Scots
and schoolmasters have a belief in retribution stronger
than that of Italians and Englishmen and playwrights,
that Henryson was the retributive kind of Scotsman and
schoolmaster, and that the spirit of the poem is in any
sense a spirit of retribution. It is filled with pity. Indeed
what Sir Herbert brings out so convincingly is that the
poem is a more humanly satisfying end to the story than
either of the earlier versions had provided, and exhibits a
profound humanity which will not rest content with anything less, as the crown of the story, than a genuine
reconciliation of the heart. In seeking this reconciliation
through retribution Henryson was no more peculiarly
Scottish than in refraining from doing so Chaucer was
peculiarly English, or Boccaccio peculiarly Italian. This
is not a matter of nationality. It would be superfluous to
labour the point if there were not a sort of conspiracy to
make Henryson a bleak and harsh writer, if Miss Agnes
Mure Mackenzie had not called *The Testament* stern, and
other critics had not cited it as a proof that the Scots have

always been dour and harsh in their human judgments. As well call Dante harsh for his treatment of Francesca, or Shakespeare dour for having Desdemona and Cordelia murdered.

The keynote of the poem is sympathy, as Sir Herbert Grierson points out, not judgment, though its theme is judgment. But the judgment is transformed when it is accepted by Cresseid in a moment of realisation; and that, indeed, is what brings about the reconciliation of which Sir Herbert speaks. Henryson's humanity is clear from the beginning of the poem; perhaps indeed humanity is a better word to describe his temper than sympathy: a humanity so simple that it needs only the most ordinary words to give it utterance, the more ordinary the better. He sees misfortune, not guilt, in Cresseid's conduct after she was turned away by Diomede:

> Than desolait scho walkit up and doun,
> And sum men sayis into the Court commoun.

He pities her 'mischance' when she was forced to

> go amang the Greikis air and lait
> Sa gigotlike, takand thy foull plesance!
> I have pietie thou suld fall sic mischance.

He interposes his charity between her and her accusers:

> Yet nevertheless quhat ever men deme or say
> In scornefull language of thy brukkilness,
> I sall excuse, as far furth as I may,
> Thy womanheid, thy wisdome and fairness;
> The quhilk Fortun has put to sic distres
> As hir plesit, and nothing throw the gilt
> Of the, throw wickit language to be spilt.

He attributes Cresseid's misfortunes and faults to chance, and absolves her of all guilt; and this is the assumption running through the poem. He does not bring her to judgment, as some critics have implied; he shows the judgment of fate and of her own heart overtaking her. His humanity in dealing with her is perfectly simple, but its simplicity contains this surprise.

It is this simple and yet surprising humanity that brings about the finest effects of style in the poem; I mean those lines which seem at once the result of exquisite poetic judgment and of a humanity so obvious that it has become sure of itself and seizes at once the ultimate situation, formulating it in the fewest possible words, words which seem just adequate and no more, and in that appear to achieve a more secure finality: all that might have been said being made superfluous by the few simple words that are said. When Cresseid is stricken with leprosy and goes to her father for comfort, Henryson leaves one line to tell of their grief:

> *Thus was thair cair aneuch betwix thame twane.*

In Cresseid's Complaint one line suffices to draw the contrast between her present and her former condition:

> *Quhair is thy Chalmer wantounlie besene?*

The incident of Troilus' meeting with her at a corner as he returns to Troy from fighting the Greeks is itself a compressed summary of the tragic situation, and is contained in three lines:

> *Than upon him scho kest up baith hir Ene,*
> *And with ane blenk it come into his thocht,*
> *That he sumtime hir face befoir had sene.*

When she is told by her companions who it was that stopped beside her and threw a purse of gold in her lap, she compresses her fault into the cry:

> *'O fals Cresseid and trew Knicht Troilus!'*

Troilus, after hearing of her misfortunes and her death,

seems again to be saying all that can be said when he exclaims:

> '*I can no moir.*
> *Scho was untrew, and wo is me thairfoir.*'

The epitaph which he inscribes on her tomb is in the same high concise style:

> *Lo, fair Ladyis, Crisseid, of Troyis toun,*
> *Sumtyme countit the flour of Womanheid,*
> *Under this stane lait Lipper lyis deid.*

No other Scottish poet has risen to this high and measured style, and Henryson himself does not attain it often, though he does as often as the subject requires it. Yet it is a style which one would have expected to suit the Scottish genius, with its seriousness and its love of compressed utterance. And that it does suit that genius is proved by Scottish folk-poetry, and particularly by the Ballads, with their complete seriousness and their extreme compression. But this gift, which belongs to the Scottish people, ceased after Henryson to belong to Scottish poets. Seriousness, though not compression, went for a long time into theology, a theology which was never more than mediocre. To the poet was left only a sort of secondary, official seriousness, that of

> *Man was made to mourn*

and

> *But pleasures are like poppies spread.*

The Scottish poets followed the tradition of Dunbar, who expressed the exuberance, wildness and eccentricity of the Middle Ages, not that of Henryson, who inherited the medieval completeness and harmony, and the power to see life whole, without taking refuge in the facetious and the grotesque. Yet Henryson embodies more strikingly than any poet who has lived since the fundamental seriousness, humanity and strength of the Scottish imagination.

'ROYAL MAN'

Notes on the tragedies of George Chapman

CHAPMAN'S virtues and faults are both excessive, and are combined in such a way that the faults seem to heighten the virtues, and the virtues to stiffen the faults. He erects his imperfections into principles, and keeps them erect by an act of will. When he succeeds he achieves an elevation beyond what seems possible, and when he fails, collapses into fantastic bathos. His mark is excess, itself a fault which he had seen splendidly displayed in Marlowe, the poet of his time whom he admired most. In Marlowe it is a quality of desire and imagination; in Chapman, of character and will. He is excessive on moral grounds, and because he believes that 'royal man' should be excessive.

> *Your mind, you say, kept in your flesh's bounds,*
> *Shows that man's will must ruled be by his power,*
> *When by true doctrine, you are taught to live*
> *Rather without the body, than within,*
> *And rather to your God still than yourself;*
> *To live to him, is to do all things fitting*
> *His image, in which, like himself, we live;*
> *To be his image, is to do those things*
> *That make us deathless, which by death is only;*
> *Doing those deeds that fit eternity;*
> *And those deeds are the perfecting the justice*
> *That makes the world last. . . .*

Chapman is not interested in human nature, or in practical morality, or in evil, but in the man of excessive virtue or spirit or pride. His tragedies show us one great figure and a crowd of nobodies who succeed somehow in destroying him. We do not believe in their power to do this until it is done, for the conflict is between a man of flesh and blood larger than life and puppets of cardboard. Yet the hero's death is real; so that we involuntarily think of it as self-inflicted or as brought about by some power outside the drama, the acts of the other characters being incapable of accounting for it. The death of Bussy D'Ambois and of Byron have, therefore, a sacrificial quality; we seem to be watching the pursuit and destruction of 'royal man' by an invisible hunter. But we see them simultaneously merely as men who ignore the limitations of human life and are bound to destroy themselves; and their ostensible betrayers, the Montsurrys and La Fins—minuses whose very names seem unreal—can only look on and ratify the foregone verdict. These heroes really exist in another dimension from the rest of the characters, and have a different reality from the action in which they are involved. They wander about, like Chapman himself, enclosed in a dream of greatness and breathing the air of that dream.

It is in these remarkable figures that the dramatic interest resides, for they are conscious of another drama beyond the drama which is shown on the stage, and lift us up into it. In their great speeches they employ a language which is not meant for the other actors; they really talk to themselves, or address an imaginary audience outside the play. Chapman is not interested—except in one or two of his comedies—in character or even in action. He employs action merely to display the soul in one of those supreme crises where action itself seems to become irrelevant, since it has done all that it can do, has come to its end, and can be disregarded. He is concerned solely with the crisis as a thing in itself, for in the crisis the real drama of his heroes is born and they rise into their own world; he therefore tries to reach it without the wearisome labour of working towards it through a methodical arrangement of situations. We can feel his impatience to arrive at those places where the souls of his heroes can expand to their full range, places on the frontier-line between life and death, time and eternity, where all terms seem to become absolute. Consequently a situation which to other tragic figures would bring despair or resignation, merely evokes new potentialities in his heroes, as if it were the opportunity for which they had been waiting. In a sense, therefore, his tragic scenes transcend tragedy, or fail to reach it; for death is merely the final assurance of immortality to his heroes. They always possess this assurance; it is one of their distinguishing marks; but it grows stronger the nearer death comes. In their death the dimension of tragedy expands to include an extra one which is not quite compatible with it, for in dying they conduct us a little distance into their own immortality. They look into that, not backwards at their destruction, except in the elegiac mood in which one may grieve for something that has happened in the past to oneself, or to a friend, or to some legendary figure in a book. The tragedies end in this way because Chapman is concerned with the soul as he conceives it, and with hardly anything else.

This exclusive concern with the soul rather than with the way in which people behave makes him an erratic moralist. His judgments of conduct are sometimes strange and almost incomprehensible, the judgments of a man who is not interested in action, either on the stage or in the ordinary world. The action in a play is the prime means for bringing out the moral character of the actors and the moral significance of the situation. We do not come to know Bussy or Byron morally, as we know Macbeth and

Hamlet, for the action has no real effect on them, since they live in a different world from the other characters, and are a law to themselves.

> There is no danger to a man that knows
> What life and death is; there's not any law
> Exceeds his knowledge; neither is it lawful
> That he should stoop to any other law.
> He goes before them, and commands them all,
> That to himself is a law rational.

In a play, which is a pattern of action and interaction, there must be an implicit standard of judgment applied to all the characters and running through the whole, otherwise its progress is confused and dislocated. Chapman's tragedies are full of such dislocations; sometimes we cannot even guess at the standard by which he judges the action; we find such monstrosities as the scene in the first act of *The Tragedy of Bussy D'Ambois*, where Bussy pays court to the Duchess of Guise in the fustian of a low actor, and insults the Duke so obscurely that one can scarcely make out what he means. It is a scene of fantastic vulgarity, yet it draws this splendid encomium on Bussy from the King's brother:

> His great heart will not down, 'tis like the sea,
> That partly by his own internal heat,
> Partly the stars' daily and nightly motion,
> Their heat and light, and partly of the place,
> The divers frames; but chiefly by the moon,
> Bristled with surges, never will be won,
> (No, not when th' hearts of all those powers are burst)
> To make retreat into his settled home,
> Till he be crowned with his own quiet foam.

There is no proportion between these lines and the conduct which inspires them; and there is little connection in *The Tragedy of Bussy D'Ambois* as a whole: here and there fine dramatic touches which come and go, but leave the characters and the action as they were. When the end does come, after these fits and starts, it comes abruptly, we scarcely know how.

Chapman's figures therefore stick out of the play, or rather burst through it, making havoc of the dramatic machinery and fixing our eyes upon them amid the ruins. Once there, they speak unencumbered in Chapman's own voice, a voice habitually choked by a consciousness of things too great for ordinary utterance and requiring the explosive power of some portent to liberate it. These mouthpieces of Chapman are images of man in his original virtue; there is nothing else quite like them in English literature. The sources from which he might have derived them are obvious enough—his long familiarity with the Homeric heroes, his absorption in Roman history and Senecan tragedy, his knowledge of the lives of some of the Renaissance princes, who attempted so many things which had seemed unthinkable before, and are described by Burckhardt. But the image into which his imagination melted those various conceptions of 'royal man' is striking and original. The French King, speaking of Bussy, gives the most complete idea of it:

> *Cousin Guise, I wonder*
> *Your honour'd disposition brooks so ill*
> *A man so good, that only would uphold*
> *Man in his native noblesse, from whose fall*
> *All our dimensions rise; that in himself*
> *(Without the outward patches of our frailty,*
> *Riches and honour) knows he comprehends*
> *Worth with the greatest; kings had never borne*
> *Such boundless empire over other men,*
> *Had all maintain'd the spirit and state of D'Ambois;*
> *Nor had the full impartial hand of nature*
> *That all things gave in her original,*
> *Without these definite terms of mine and thine,*
> *Been turn'd unjustly to the hand of Fortune,*

26

Had all preserved her in her prime, like D'Ambois;
No envy, no disjunction had dissolved
Or pluck'd one stick out of the golden faggot
In which the world of Saturn bound our lives,
Had all been held together with the nerves,
The genius, and th' ingenuous soul of D'Ambois.

The idea that if man had not fallen there would be no kings or subjects, no mine or thine, recurs in the tragedies, and evokes an image which cannot be described either as a new ideal of society or as a new state of being. Bussy D'Ambois and Byron are unfallen men among the fallen, but their virtues are not Adam's; they are not equipped with innocence, but with native noblesse, spirit and state, genius and an ingenuous soul, the virtues of the Renaissance. Bussy is like a cross between Adam and Achilles crossed again by something quite different, the Renaissance man stepping out of the Middle Ages into a new world. There is something legendary in this figure, out of which Chapman might have created the myth of his age if he had possessed greater dramatic power and a less erratic genius. The legendary quality appears more clearly in the description of Byron sitting his horse:

Your Majesty hath miss'd a royal sight:
The Duke Byron, on his brave beast Pastrana,
Who sits him like a full-sail'd argosy,
Danced with a lofty billow, and as snug
Plies to his bearer, both their motions mix'd;
And being consider'd in their site together
They do the best present the state of man
In his first royalty ruling, and of beasts
In their first loyalty serving; one commanding,
And no way being moved; the other serving,
And no way being compell'd; of all the sights
That ever my eyes witness'd; and they make
A doctrinal and witty hieroglyphic
Of a blest kingdom; to express and teach,

Kings to command as they could serve, and subjects
To serve as if they had power to command.

'A doctrinal and witty hieroglyphic of a blest kingdom': this is the hypothesis on which the real drama of Chapman's heroes is grounded, an action elevated above the ostensible action. This blest kingdom is not set in the past, a mere recollection of the Golden Age, nor in the future, a prophecy of a coming society, but rather in a perpetual present apprehended and to that degree lived in by the hero, the unfallen man. We accept this hero and his drama as real, perhaps because with one part of him man still lives in the world before the Fall, and with another in the world after it, since the Fall—assuming that it stands for anything in human experience—is not a historical event but something which is always happening. Chapman's heroes exist more largely in the world before the Fall than any other figures in tragedy; it is for this reason that they are so clearly conscious of their immortality; for this reason, too, perhaps, that they are so awkward and clumsy in the world of action: we could hardly expect adroitness and expedience from these men existing

In all the free-born powers of royal man.

It is not, then, the world in which they move, but the world we see through their eyes which gives Chapman's heroes their greatness. Their nature demands two things from that world created in their image: freedom and glory, but not power or love. In almost any page of the tragedies we find proofs of Chapman's possession by these qualities:

Hot, shining, swift, light, and aspiring things
Are of immortal and celestial nature. . . .
To fear a violent good, abuseth goodness;
'Tis immortality to die aspiring,
As if a man were taken quick to heaven;
What will not hold perfection, let it burst. . . .

28

I'll wear those golden spurs upon my heels,
And kick at fate; be free, all worthy spirits,
And stretch yourselves, for greatness and for height. . . .

This aspiring life just touching the earth and perpetually mounting into the air is suggested finely in his descriptions of his heroes fighting:

Like bonfires of contributory wood
Every man's look show'd, fed with others' spirit. . . .

D'Ambois (that like a laurel put on fire
Sparkled and spit). . . .

And then like flame and powder they commixt
So spritely, that I wish'd they had been spirits. . . .

He turn'd wild lightning in the lackeys' hands. . . .

their saucy fingers
Flew as too hot off, as he had been fire. . . .

The battles then in two half-moons enclosed him,
In which he showed as if he were the light,
And they but earth. . . .

These combats are not kindled and fed by merely human passion; they are like an explosion of the elements into speed and fire, impersonal, non-human, transmuting the fighting heroes into those

Hot, shining, swift, light, and aspiring things

which to Chapman were of immortal and celestial nature. In a well-known passage Clermont D'Ambois, Bussy's brother, says:

And know ye all (though far from all your aims,
Yet worth them all, and all men's endless studies)
That in this one thing, all the discipline
Of manners, and of manhood is contain'd;

A man to join himself with th' Universe,
In his main sway, and make (in all things fit)
One with that all, and go on, round as it. . . .

Clermont is expounding a high philosophical idea; but
there are more ways of joining oneself with the universe
than those he lays down, and Chapman's heroes inevitably
make for that junction, whether in battle or in speculation
or in death. Bussy's last speech calls up a gigantic vision
of his memory being taken into the keeping of universal
nature:

The equal thought I bear of life and death
Shall make me faint on no side; I am up;
Here like a Roman statue I will stand
Till death hath made me marble; oh, my fame,
Live in despite of murder; take thy wings
And haste thee where the grey-eyed morn perfumes
Her rosy chariot with Sabaean spices,
Fly, where the evening from th' Iberian vales,
Takes on her swarthy shoulder Hecate,
Crowned with a grove of oaks; fly where men feel
The cunning axletree; and those that suffer
Beneath the chariot of the snowy Bear:
And tell them all that D'Ambois now is hasting
To the eternal dwellers. . . .

There is no other last speech like that in Elizabethan
drama. 'Oh, my fame, live in despite of murder' recalls
Hamlet's wish that his memory might be vindicated; but
Hamlet does not confide it to the universe, but to Horatio,
mortal like himself:

If thou didst ever hold me in thy heart,
Absent thee from felicity awhile,
And in this harsh world draw thy breath in pain,
To tell my story.

The difference is great, the difference between an imagination which penetrates deep into human life, and one which
is concentrated upon a great idea. The essential thing

about Chapman's heroes, as about Marlowe's, is that they
are framed of the four elements, not that they are human
beings obliged to live somehow with other human beings;
they are nearer to earth, water, air and fire than to us as we
know ourselves. Marlowe gives the concoction from which
Chapman's heroes were drawn:

> *Nature that fram'd us of four elements,*
> *Warring within our breasts for regiment,*
> *Doth teach us all to have aspiring minds.*

For Marlowe's poetry, too, like Chapman's, is inspired
by a philosophical idea of man, not by human life as the
observer sees it. His idea at first seems to be much the
same as Chapman's, but in reality is very different; for
though like Chapman he is in love with freedom and
glory, he is also in love with their rewards, with

> *the ripest fruit of all*
> *That perfect bliss and sole felicity,*
> *The sweet fruition of an earthly crown.*

Chapman's heroes have no ambition to achieve an
earthly crown. They love freedom and glory disinteres-
tedly as states of the soul, for their own and for the soul's
sake. Their aspiring minds reach for a state in which
freedom and glory are possessed purely, without admix-
ture, as things in themselves. Bussy does not try to gain
power over others, but merely to live after the pattern of
'royal man'. Byron is drawn into plots against his king,
but his hostility is nothing more than that of a man who
feels he is a king against another who merely is one. His
plots bring him to the scaffold; they also precipitate his
spiritual tragedy, for he can no longer enjoy freedom and
glory in their purity after he has yielded to private ambition and envy. He is an unfallen man who yields to the
persuasions of the fallen and becomes one of them, greater

than them still, but no longer different from them. He loses his native noblesse by trying to win the noblesse of this world.

We do not come to know Bussy and Byron morally, for they are never affected by the action, never tested by it; but we do come to know what morality is—or what morality is to Chapman—through their mouths. That morality is a passionate, disinterested devotion to freedom and glory, the

Doing those deeds that fit eternity.

Chapman carried his idea of freedom and glory to excess, no doubt, but excess was at the root of his virtues.

Since I am free,
(Offending no just law), let no law make
By any wrong it does, my life her slave:
When I am wrong'd, and that law fails to right me,
Let me be king myself (as man was made),
And do a justice that exceeds the law.

Chapman's conception of morality is partial: in concentrating on greatness it pays little attention to goodness. But it is disinterested; it rises above the very thought of expediency, and takes us into the region of absolute things.

THE POLITICS OF *KING LEAR*[1]

DURING the past few weeks I have been reading every now and then the collected essays of the great teacher and scholar in whose memory these lectures are held. They delighted but daunted me; for the massive equipment of learning which is handled in them with such ease is far beyond my command. I have come to books when I could, in the intervals of a life spent on other things, many of them not of my choosing; books have not been my occupation. But I console myself with the thought that every critic, however learned, must— for he cannot help it—bring to his interpretation of works of imagination not only his reading, but his life, the experiences he has passed through, the emotions he has felt, the reflections he has made upon them, even the accidents and trivialities of every day, since they are all parts of life and help us, therefore, to comprehend the poet's image of life.

In what I say to-day I do not intend to touch upon the more profound aspects of *King Lear*, though I hope my argument may have some reference to them. I want to speak of the politics of the play, and these naturally must have some relation to Shakespeare's politics. That, of course, is a difficult problem, and a great deal has been written about it by critics ancient and modern, from Coleridge to the late John Palmer and Dr. Tillyard in his last two volumes. I shall not try to summarise the arguments of these writers. But one point is crucial, and has

[1] The W. P. Ker lecture for 1946, given in the University of Glasgow

been brought up repeatedly, and I should like to say a few words about it. Briefly, it has been maintained that Shakespeare had no politics. Now this may be true in a sense, if it means that he cannot be put down either as a Conservative, or a Liberal, or a Socialist, or whatever the counterparts of these modern classifications were in his time. I shall not use these terms, or adopt Swinburne's opinion that *King Lear* is the work of Shakespeare the Socialist: Swinburne was speaking rhetorically. But a man may have political sense, and political sense of a high kind, without falling into any of these categories; for his mind, while working politically, may not think in terms of any of them. To say that Shakespeare had no politics—if one takes the statement seriously—can only mean that he had no conception of what is good in society; and to assert that would bring an immediate denial from everybody. It has been said that he was above the conflict; it would be more true to say that he was above the classification. For he had very strongly a conception of what is good in society, just as he had very strongly a sense of what is good in conduct. Professor Caroline Spurgeon demonstrates this in her analysis of the Histories; but it seems to me that the play in which it is most clearly evident is *King Lear*.

To understand the Tragedies and the Histories one has to keep in mind the historical background of Shakespeare's age. I cannot attempt to describe that background, and must indicate it in a sort of historical shorthand by enumerating a few dates. The Dissolution of the Monasteries, which rang the warning that the old medieval order was nearing its end, was completed in 1539, twenty-five years before Shakespeare's birth. *King Lear* was written round about 1605–6, six or seven years after the birth of Cromwell and forty-three before the execution of Charles I. In the interval between the first and the last of these dates the medieval world with its communal tradition was dying, and the modern individualist world was bringing itself to birth. Shakespeare lived in that violent period of transition. The old world still echoed in his ears; he was aware of the new as we are aware of the future, that is as an inchoate, semi-prophetic dream. Now it seems to me that that dream, those echoes, fill *King Lear* and help to account for the sense of vastness which it gives us, the feeling that it covers a far greater stretch of time than can be explained by the action. The extreme age of the King brings to our minds the image of a civilisation of legendary antiquity; yet that civilisation is destroyed by a new generation which belongs to Shakespeare's own time, a perfectly up-to-date gang of Renaissance adventurers. The play contains, therefore, or has taken on, a significance which Shakespeare probably could not have known, and without his being aware, he wrote in it the mythical drama of the transmutation of civilisation. One is reminded of the scene in the second part of Goethe's *Faust* where the temples of the ancient world change and crumble and rise again in the towering Gothic structures of the Middle Ages.

Of the great tragedies *King Lear* is the only one in which two ideas of society are directly confronted, and the old generation and the new are set face to face, each assured of its own right to power. *Macbeth* is a drama of murder and usurpation and remorse; it changes the succession of the crown and brings guilt upon the offender, the guilt showing that the old order is still accepted, and the old laws still valid, since Macbeth feels that he has done wrong both as the killer of a man and the supplanter of a king. But Regan, Goneril and Cornwall never feel that they have done wrong, and this is because they represent a new idea; and new ideas, like everything new, bring with them their own kind of innocence. *Hamlet*, although it deals with a dynastic and therefore a political problem, is essentially a personal drama, perhaps the most personal of them all: there is no relationship in *King Lear* so intensely intimate as that of Hamlet to his mother. Lear's own relation to his daughters is most nearly so; yet Goneril and Regan are curiously equal in his estimation, indeed almost interchangeable; he is willing to accept either if she will only take his part against her sister; and as if his rage had blotted out their very names, he confounds them indistinguishably in his curses upon his daughters; so that we feel that daughters have become to him some strange and monstrous species. For Goneril and Regan, on the other hand, he is hardly even a father, but merely an old man who thinks and feels in a way they cannot understand, and is a burden to them. The almost impersonal equivalence of the two women in their father's eyes gives a cast to the play which is not to be found in any of the others, and makes us feel, indeed, that Lear is not contending with ordinary human beings but with mere forces to which any human appeal is vain, since it is not even capable of evoking a response. He, the representative of the old, is confronted with something brand new; he cannot understand it, and it does not even care to understand him.

There is something more, then, than ingratitude in the reaction of Lear's daughters, though the ingratitude, that 'marble-hearted fiend', strikes most deeply into his heart. This something more is their attitude to power, which is grounded on their attitude to life. It is this, more than the ingratitude, that estranges Lear from them. His appeals cannot reach them, but, worse still, his mind cannot understand them, no matter how hard he tries. As this attitude of his daughters violates all his ideas of the nature of things, it seems to him against nature, so that he can only cry out against them as 'unnatural hags'. 'Unnatural' is the nearest he can come to a definition of the unbridgeable distance that divides him from them; his real struggle is to annihilate that distance, but he never succeeds; in his most intimate conflict with them he never comes any closer to them. When Regan shuts him out in the storm her action is symbolical as well as practical. His daughters are inside; he is outside. They are in two different worlds.

The story of *King Lear* tells how an old man parts his kingdom between his daughters when he feels no longer able to rule. He retains to himself only

The name and all the additions to a king,

and leaves to them and their husbands

The sway, revenue, execution of the rest.

His daughters, having got what they want, that is the power, and not caring much for the name or the additions, turn against him. As daughters, their act is one of filial ingratitude; as princesses and vice-regents, it is an act of 'revolt and flying off'. These two aspects of their policy are inseparable; in turning against their father they subvert the kingdom; by the same deed they commit two crimes, one private and one public.

But there is a complication. For Goneril and Regan's idea of rulership is different from their father's, and so, on the anguish caused by their ingratitude, is piled the bewilderment of one who feels he is dealing with creatures whose notions are equally incomprehensible to his heart and his mind. In the later stages of the conflict it is the tortures of his mind that become the most unbearable, since they make the nature of things incomprehensible to him, and confound his ideas in a chaos from which the only escape is madness. The note of Lear's tragedy is to be found in another play:

Chaos is come again.

The note of the play itself, the summary judgment on the whole action, is expressed in Albany's words:

> *If that the heavens do not their visible spirits*
> *Send quickly down to tame these vile offences*
> *It will come,*
> *Humanity must perforce prey on itself,*
> *Like monsters of the deep.*

Yet this is the world which Lear's two daughters and Cornwall and Edmund and Oswald freely accept as theirs; it is their idea of a brand-new order; and the play therefore deals not only with a conflict between two daughters and their father, and two vice-regents and their king, but with two conceptions of society.

In the new conception of society, that of Goneril and Regan, nature plays an important part; the number of references to nature in the play, almost always as images of cruelty or horror, has often been commented upon. Bradley in his book on Shakespearean tragedy tries to make a list of the lower animals which are mentioned in the drama, a list which had afterwards to be completed by Professor Spurgeon. 'These references are broadcast through the whole play', he says, 'as though Shakespeare's mind were so busy with the subject that he could hardly write a page without some allusion to it. The dog, the horse, the cow, the sheep, the hog, the lion, the bear, the wolf, the fox, the monkey, the pole-cat, the civet-cat, the pelican, the owl, the crow, the chough, the wren, the fly, the butterfly, the rat, the mouse, the frog, the tadpole, the wall-newt, the water-newt, the worm—I am sure I cannot have completed the list, and some of them are mentioned again and again. . . . Sometimes a person in the drama is compared, openly or implicitly, with one of them. Goneril is a kite; her ingratitude has a serpent tooth: she has struck her father most serpentlike upon the very heart: her visage is wolfish: she has tied sharp-toothed unkindness like a vulture on her father's breast: for her husband she is a gilded serpent: to Gloster her cruelty seems to have the fangs of a boar. She and Regan are dog-hearted: they are tigers, not daughters; each is an adder to the other; the flesh of each is covered with the fell of a beast. . . . As we read, the souls of all the beasts in turn seem to us to have entered the bodies of these mortals; horrible in their venom, savagery, lust, deceitfulness, sloth, cruelty, filthiness.'

After looking on this picture of nature, turn to the first speech of Edmund, the mouthpiece of the new generation:

> *Thou, Nature, art my goddess; to thy law*
> *My services are bound. Wherefore should I*
> *Stand in the plague of custom, and permit*
> *The curiosity of nations to deprive me,*
> *For that I am some twelve or fourteen moonshines*
> *Lag of a brother? Why bastard? wherefore base?*
> *When my dimensions are as well compact,*
> *My mind as generous, and my shape as true,*
> *As honest madman's issue? Why brand they us*
> *With base? with baseness? bastardy? base, base?*
> *Who in the lusty stealth of nature take*
> *More composition and fierce quality*
> *Than doth, within a dull, stale, tired bed,*
> *Go to the creating a whole tribe of fops,*
> *Got 'tween asleep and wake? Well then,*
> *Legitimate Edgar, I must have your land:*
> *Our father's love is to the bastard Edmund*
> *As to the legitimate. Fine word, 'legitimate'!*

Goneril and Regan and Cornwall, though they do not have Edmund's imaginative intellect, worship nature in the same spirit. For it gives them the freedom they hunger for, absolves them from the plague of custom, justifies them when they reflect that their dimensions are well-compact and their shape true, as if that were all that was needed to make human a creature in human shape. They rely confidently on certain simple facts of nature: that they are young and their father old, strong while he is infirm, and that their youth and strength give them a short cut to their desires. They are so close to the state of nature that they hardly need to reflect: what they have the power to do they claim the right to do. Or rather the power and its expression in action are almost simultaneous. When Lear pleads with Goneril she replies:

> *Be then desired*
> *By her, that else will take the thing she begs,*
> *A little to disquantity your train.*

Regan says a little later:

> *I pray you, father, being weak, seem so.*

After Cornwall puts out Gloster's eyes, and Regan stabs the servant who tried to prevent it, he says:

> *Turn out that eyeless villain; throw this slave*
> *Upon the dunghill.*

And Regan adds:

> *Go thrust him out at gates, and let him smell*
> *His way to Dover.*

The most repulsive thing about these words, apart from their cruelty, is their triteness. The two daughters ignore all the complexities of what to them is merely a situation, and solve it at once by an abominable truism. They are quite rational, but only on the lowest plane of reason, and they have that contempt for other ways of thinking which comes from a knowledge of their own efficiency. As they are rational, they have a good conscience, even a touch of self-righteousness; they sincerely believe their father is in the wrong and they are in the right, since they conceive they know the world as it is, and act in conformity with it, the source of all effective power. They do not see far, but they see clearly. When they reflect, and take thought for the future, their decisions are rational and satisfactory by their own standards. When Goneril wants an excuse for reducing her father's retinue, she instructs her servant Oswald how to behave towards him:

> *Put on what weary negligence you please,*
> *You and your fellows; I'd have it come to question . . .*
> *And let his knights have colder looks among you;*
> *What grows of it, no matter; advise your fellows so:*
> *I would breed from hence occasions, and I shall,*
> *That I may speak.*

The members of the new generation are bound together by common interest, since they all wish to succeed in their individual ambitions, which they cannot achieve without each other's help; but their most immediate bond is a common way of thinking, a spontaneous intellectual affinity resembling that of a chosen group to whom a new vision of the world has been vouchsafed. They feel they are of the elect and have the sense of superiority which fits their station. Yet they are irresistibly driven to choose as confederates men and women of their own stamp, even though these are likely in the long run to thwart or destroy them. Having renounced morality as a useful factor in conduct, they judge others with a total lack of moral discrimination, being confined irretrievably to the low plane of reason on which they move. Accordingly Cornwall can say to Edmund:

> *You shall be ours;*
> *Natures of such deep trust we shall much need;*
> *You we first seize on.*

And of honest Kent:

> *This is some fellow,*
> *Who, having been praised for bluntness, doth affect*
> *A saucy roughness, and constrains the garb*

Quite from his nature; he cannot flatter, he,
An honest mind and plain, he must speak truth:
An they will take it, so; if not, he's plain.
These kind of knaves I know, which in this plainness
Harbour more craft and more corrupter ends
Than twenty silly-ducking observants,
That stretch their duties nicely.

Lear could not have made these mistakes, for he had some knowledge of the moral nature of man; but Cornwall and Goneril and Regan can and do; for while they have worked out the equation of life with complete satisfaction to themselves, they have done so by omitting what gives life meaning.

The new generation may be regarded then as the embodiment of wickedness, a wickedness of that special kind which I have tried to indicate. But can it also be said that they represent a new conception of society? If we had not lived through the last twenty years, had not seen the rise of Fascism in Italy and Germany and Communism in Russia, and did not know the theory and practice by which they were upheld, we might be disposed to deny this. As it is we cannot. We know, too, that Shakespeare was acquainted with the Renaissance man, and that his plays abound in references to 'policy', which stood in his time for what the Germans dignify by the name of *Realpolitik*; that is, political action which ignores all moral considerations. In Burckhardt's account of the lives of the Roman *condottieri* there is ground enough for believing that figures like Goneril and Regan could both behave as they did and rule a state. It was an age in which Italian princes, and others too, permitted themselves a liberty of action which one would have expected to disrupt or destroy the state; yet it did not. Instead, the subject conformed to a rulership which seemed impossible because anti-social; he conformed by becoming the mere instrument of his ruler.

The Macchiavellian became a stock figure in later Elizabethan drama; Shakespeare must have met many a man
like Edmund who refused to be deprived by the plague of
custom. Bradley calls Edmund a mere adventurer, yet
afterwards describes him as a consummate politician in the
new style. 'He acts in pursuance of a purpose', says
Bradley, 'and if he has any affections or dislikes, ignores
them. He is determined to make his way, first to his
brother's lands, then—as the prospect widens—to the
crown; and he regards men and women, with their virtues
and vices, together with the bonds of kinship, friendship,
or allegiance, merely as hindrances or helps to his end.
They are for him divested of all quality except for their
relation to his end; as indifferent as mathematical quan-
tities or mere physical agents.

> *A credulous father, and a brother noble,*
> *. . . I see the business,*

he says, as if he were talking of *x* and *y*.'

To regard things in this way is to see them in a continuous present divested of all associations, denuded of
memory and the depth which memory gives to life. Goneril
and Regan, even more than Edmund, exist in this shallow
present, and it is to them a present in both senses of the
word, a gift freely given into their hands to do with what
they like. Having no memory, they have no responsibility,
and no need, therefore, to treat their father differently
from any other troublesome old man. This may simply be
another way of saying that they are evil, for it may be that
evil consists in a hiatus in the soul, a craving blank, a lack
of one of the essential threads which bind experience into
a coherent whole and give it a consistent meaning. The
hiatus in Lear's daughters is specifically a hiatus of
memory, a breach in continuity; they seem to come from

43

nowhere and to be on the way to nowhere; they have words and acts only to meet the momentary emergency, the momentary appetite; their speech is therefore strikingly deficient in imagery, and consists of a sequence of pitiless truisms. Bradley complains of the characters in the play that, 'Considered simply as psychological studies few of them are of the highest interest'. This is true of Goneril and Regan, for the human qualities of highest interest are left out of them. But that was Shakespeare's intention; he had to interest us in two characters who were both evil and shallow. Their shallowness is ultimately that of the Macchiavellian view of life as it was understood in his age, of 'policy', or *Realpolitik*, whichever we may choose to call it. The sisters are harpies, but as rulers they act in the approved contemporary Macchiavellian convention. If we read Burckhardt, if we reflect that Macchiavellianism was a current preoccupation in Shakespeare's time, and consider further that the Renaissance gave to the individual a prominence he had not possessed since classical times, and that personal power, especially in princes, appeared sometimes to be boundless, we need not shrink from regarding Edmund and his confederates as political types. Poets of Shakespeare's time had espoused the liberated hero, the glorious individual, among them Marlowe, and Chapman with his ideal of 'royal man'. But Shakespeare did not: his political sense put him on the opposite side.

To understand his attitude to the new generation we must finally consider his identification of them with nature. Their life in the moment, their decisions based on what the mere moment presents, their want of continuity, their permanent empty newness, are sufficient in themselves to involve them with nature, for nature is always new and has no background; it is society that is old. Their position may be defined by saying that they claim a liberty which is proper to nature but not to society. This is what makes them in a sense unnatural; and this is what makes it impossible for Lear with his traditional beliefs to understand them. Nature is not corrupt in itself, nor is man as Shakespeare normally sees him; but when man is swallowed up in nature a result is produced which seems to corrupt both. Goneril, Regan and Cornwall become mere animals furnished with human faculties which they have stolen, not inherited by right. Words are their teeth and claws, and action the technique of the deadly spring. It may be that this new freedom, the freedom of nature not of civilised humanity, pointed to the development which society was to follow, to *laissez-faire* and the struggle for existence and the survival of the fittest so dear to the Victorian economists: but I have no time to follow it there.

Against this idea of society what had Lear to set? His conception is nowhere clearly formulated, for it is old, and it is to him the accepted conception. But in almost everything he says, whether in anger or kindness, we can feel what it is: he sets against the idea of natural freedom the sacred tradition of human society. His attitude to nature when he is in his right mind is quite objective:

> *Allow not nature more than nature needs,*
> *Man's life is cheap as beast's.*

He himself does not turn to nature for help until his folly is let in and his dear judgment out, and then he asks her, the terrible goddess, to fulfil his curse on Goneril:

> *If she must teem,*
> *Create her child of spleen, that it may live*
> *To be a thwart disnatured torment to her!*
> *Let it stamp wrinkles in her brow of youth,*
> *With cadent tears fret channels in her cheeks,*
> *Turn all her mother's pains and benefits*
> *To laughter and contempt, that she may feel*

> *How sharper than a serpent's tooth it is*
> *To have a thankless child!*

Later, when his mind is tortured by the problem of his daughters' insensibility, his speculations on nature take on a darker colour:

> Then let them anatomize Regan, see what breeds about her heart. Is there any cause in nature that makes these hard hearts?

The more forlorn his state becomes, the more he feels the indifference and cruelty of nature even in small things:

> *The little dogs and all,*
> *Tray, Blanch, and Sweetheart, see, they bark at me.*

He sees clearly what man is in his natural state, and describes him after he meets Edgar in his rags:

> Is man no more than this? Consider him well. Thou owest the worm no silk, the beast no hide, the sheep no wool, the cat no perfume. Ha! here's three on's are sophisticated; thou art the thing itself; unaccommodated man is no more but such a poor, bare, forked animal as thou art.

Yet for Lear and his friends there exists an order of society so obviously springing from the nature and needs of man that it can also be called natural, though not in Edmund's sense. When it is subverted, the universal frame seems to be wrenched from its place, and the new chaos can be explained only as the result of a portent. Gloster argues:

> These late eclipses in the sun and moon portend no good to us: though the wisdom of nature can reason it thus and thus, yet nature finds itself scourged by the sequent effects. Love cools, friendship falls off, brothers divide: in cities, mutinies; in countries, discord; in palaces, treason; and the bond cracked 'twixt son and father. . . . We have seen the best of our time: machinations, hollowness, treachery, and all ruinous disorders follow us disquietly to our graves.

Kent exclaims:

> *It is the stars,*
> *The stars above us, govern our conditions;*
> *Else one self mate and make could not beget*
> *Such different issues.*

Gloster and Kent needed such explanations, for division between brothers, mutinies, discords, treacheries did not seem to them in accordance with the nature of society. But to Edmund this state is the natural one, for it gives him an opportunity to rise; and so he can sneer almost virtuously at his father's superstitions:

> This is the excellent foppery of the world, that, when we are sick in fortune, often the surfeit of our own behaviour, we make guilty of our disasters the sun, the moon, and the stars; as if we were villains on necessity, fools by heavenly compulsion, knaves, thieves, and treachers by spherical predominance, drunkards, liars, and adulterers by an enforced obedience of planetary influence; and all that we are evil in, by a divine thrusting on: an admirable evasion of whoremaster man, to lay his goatish disposition to the charge of a star! My father compounded with my mother under the dragon's tail, and my nativity was under *Ursa major*; so that it follows I am rough and lecherous. Fut! I should have been that I am had the maidenliest star in the firmament twinkled on my bastardizing.

Edmund can say this because he is a child of nature, and a liar, adulterer and treacher by free choice, for each furthers his advancement.

The tradition of society which Lear represents is difficult to reconstruct from anything that is said in the play. Its nature is implied in Lear's appeals to Regan:

> *'Tis not in thee*
> *To grudge my pleasures, to cut off my train,*
> *To bandy hasty words, to scant my sizes,*
> *And, in conclusion, to oppose the bolt*
> *Against my coming in: thou better know'st*
> *The offices of nature, bond of childhood,*
> *Effects of courtesy, dues of gratitude.*

47

It is to such things that Lear appeals when he is trying to find a way to his daughters. He appeals to a sentiment which to him means everything, but which to them means nothing: they do not even understand it. His conception of society can be guessed at again in the words which he says to his Fool out of his own grief:

> *Poor fool and knave, I have one part in my heart*
> *That's sorry yet for thee.*

We can guess at it again in these words which made Swinburne write of Shakespeare the Socialist:

> *Poor naked wretches, whereso'er you are,*
> *That bide the pelting of this pitiless storm,*
> *How shall your houseless heads and unfed sides,*
> *Your loop'd and window'd raggedness, defend you*
> *From seasons such as these? O! I have ta'en*
> *Too little care of this. Take physic, pomp;*
> *Expose thyself to feel what wretches feel,*
> *That thou mayst shake the superflux to them,*
> *And show the heavens more just.*

The difference between that and

> *I pray you, father, being weak, seem so,*

or

> *Go thrust him out at gates, and let him smell*
> *His way to Dover,*

is the difference between the two worlds described in the play. Lear is an imperfect king; he has taken too little care for his subjects; but he admits the obligation; and the social realities on which he relies, and to which he appeals as if they were self-evident, are purely human, not realistic in the modern sense:

> *The offices of nature, bond of childhood,*
> *Effects of courtesy, dues of gratitude.*

If we discern a conception of society behind such fragmentary utterances, and behind Lear himself, it appears to us a society bound together not by force and appetite, but by a sort of piety and human fitness, a natural piety, one would feel inclined to say, if the word were not used in the play as inimical to society.

Lear is very old, almost Saturnian in his legendary age; the kingdom in him exists as a memory and no longer as a fact; the old order lies in ruin, and the new is not an order. The communal tradition, filled with memory, has been smashed by an individualism that exists in its perpetual shallow present. The judgment on the new generation is passed by a member of it who does not belong spiritually to it: Edgar. It is remarkable that in the scenes where Lear, the Fool and Edgar are together, it is Edgar, the only sane man, who conjures up the deepest images of horror. For he is of the new generation, and knows it as Lear cannot. When Lear asks him who he is, he replies by giving a portrait of his brother Edmund:

> A servingman, proud in heart and mind; that curled my hair, wore gloves in my cap, served the lust of my mistress' heart, and did the act of darkness with her; swore as many oaths as I spake words, and broke them in the sweet face of heaven; one that slept in the contriving of lust, and waked to do it. Wine loved I deeply, dice dearly, and in woman out-paramoured the Turk: false of heart, light of ear, bloody of hand; hog in sloth, fox in stealth, wolf in greediness, dog in madness, lion in prey.

That is a picture of an animal with human faculties, made corrupt and legendary by the proudly curled hair. It is a picture, too, of the man of policy in the latest style, who regards the sacred order of society as his prey, and recognises only two realities, interest and force, the gods of the new age.

LAURENCE STERNE

'THEY order, said I, this matter better in France.'
It is one of the most perfect openings to an English
book. It sets the key of *A Sentimental Journey*, and
is like one of those themes which preordain all the forms
into which a musical composition will flow. It raises us to
the level where the book will stay; it has the force of an
incantation.

From a phrase such as this the mystery of Sterne's
operation on our minds can be realised, and almost any
other might have served as well; for his operation is the
operation of pure style. It is style that creates the world of
Tristram Shandy and *A Sentimental Journey*. In most novels
we can roughly separate form and content, treatment and
subject-matter; but in these two books they are indivisible;
there seems to be no hiatus between intention and execution. They stand on a plane of their own in English fiction,
as triumphs of reason and imagination over subject-matter.

Or Sterne's feat might be described by saying that from
beginning to end his utterance is as completely in character as the part of a great comic figure on the stage.
Nothing can disturb his inflection. He may lecture his
readers, or argue with them, or coquette with them, or
overlook them; but always he is in his part. This is the
reason why, though he is far more ubiquitous than Fielding, his presence is never intrusive. He knew that everything in a work of art must be given a reason, and he made
his position secure by making himself indispensable to
his characters. He invented for himself a void which only

his own figure could fill, so that without him we feel that Mr. Shandy, Uncle Toby, Trim and the others would remain in eternal silence and immobility, and never think of the things they say. He is their Boswell. He feeds them with curious questions and busily notes the answers, appearing at their heels as a benevolent familiar. And out of this fictitious function he contrives to charm another; that of the worried guardian. For he can never quite catch up with all his charges; he has to leave one to run after another, or soliloquise on the impossibility of attending to them all, or appeal to the reader for help. In this way he finds a host of urgent reasons for appearing in the centre of the stage; reasons absurd in themselves, perhaps, yet essential to his plan. While Fielding in his few appearances has the air of a gentlemanly intruder.

Yet this still does not do justice to Sterne. For he never appears except in his literary character, except, that is to say, as a stylised portrait of himself, imaginatively conceived like the other figures. Fielding comes on simply as the self-conscious author, or the eighteenth-century English gentleman. His gesture is as disconcerting as that of certain music-hall entertainers at the end of a turn. We know the feeling of discomfort when, after watching a figure on the stage universalised by paint and wig, a wig-less, well-groomed young man scuttles out from the wings and bows. A precious illusion is destroyed to draw attention to an ordinary fact. Fielding's introductory chapters to his books dispel the illusion by suggesting the gentleman. His pleasant manly features are presented to us, and we are expected to remember them when in the next chapter the mere novelist comes on.

Novelists have a habit of appearing at unforeseen moments in their own characters; the novel is an accommodating art and can stand it; but it is Sterne's avoidance of this vice which puts him on his own plane of perfection in English fiction. For by appearing only as his imaginative portrait in *Tristram Shandy*, he renounces the luxury of being himself; he never claims the reader's sympathies in the touching role of a human being. He is never a man, a gentleman, a husband, a father, a citizen, a clergyman. He is continuously encased in motley, and painted and wigged; every gesture and intonation is stylised; and Laurence Sterne is resolved into an imaginative sublimation of himself. This mime has of course a whole range of ideas, a whole gamut of emotions, entirely congruous with it; feels hope, disappointment, contentment, pity; laughs and cries. Yet it is not Sterne who laughs and cries, but this double which both follows the lines of its original and cancels them, like a mask. And we have only to remember that this mask is never laid aside, that it usurps entirely the place of its original, which disappears altogether, for the fabulous quality of Sterne's art to become comprehensible. Perhaps the best analogy for Sterne's masked personality can be found among Shakespeare's court jesters; he is like those half-fabulous creatures who are never out of their motley, who, we feel, are not parted from it even when they are asleep, and who will die as they have lived in it. And because the call before the curtain never comes, because the paint and the wig have grown into skin and hair, we are transported into a magical world, into a non-stop performance on the stage of some cosmic Empire or Palladium.

This is Sterne's world; it is the world also of Shakespeare's comic characters; but, except for these, few have entered it. It is a world which can be thrown open only by complete masquerade or disguise, for disguise is a magical art. It not only enables us to do things which, with our own features presented to the world, we would not permit ourselves to do, or dare not do; it not only gives us licence to be irresponsible, undignified, outspoken: it sets free in us a new personality with a suppleness and daring of movement which seems to belong to the dream-world. Sterne is the freest of English comic writers, and freest in the sense of being the readiest, the most quickly, airily and subtly moving. In that freedom thought is indistinguishable from condensed fancy, and fancy from subtilised thought. Take his description of his meeting with the French lady at Calais. He seized her hand, then it escaped him, then he captured it again.

> The pulsation of the arteries along my fingers pressing across hers, told her what was passing within me; she looked down—a silence of some moments followed. I fear, in this interval, I must have made some slight effort towards a closer compression of her hand, from a subtle sensation I felt in the palm of my own—not as if she was going to withdraw hers—but, as if she thought about it—and I had infallibly lost it a second time, had not instinct more than reason directed me to the last resource in these dangers—to hold it loosely, and as if I was every moment going to release it of myself; so she let it continue.

That is a passage which one might find in Proust, except that it is quite unlike Proust in that we cannot tell whether its exactitude is one of fancy or of observation. It moves along two routes simultaneously, and has a sort of enigmatical, interchangeable truth applicable equally to our world and a world of pure fancy. It suggests two things at once, the intellectual analysis of the modern novel, and the intellectual imagination of the metaphysical poets. Through what seems to be pure invention Donne reaches truths about experience which we feel could be reached in no other way. Through intellectual fantasy Sterne does the same thing. And, like Donne and Proust, his aim is to find the intelligible and the spiritual in minute manifestations of the physical; to bring a greater province of experience under the rule of intellectual law.

So that perhaps this licence to pause over trifling or minute things was the most valuable prerogative which the freedom of motley gave him. It allowed him to follow out at his ease processes which Fielding with his instinct for balance, and Smollett with his practical temper, would have passed over with contempt: the transmutations of the homunculus, the size of noses, Uncle Toby's groin and Widow Wadman's eye. It allowed him to show that 'preference for the windings of his own mind to the guide-book with its hammered high road', which, Virginia Woolf tells us, makes him 'singularly of our own age'. His eyes, she says again, 'were so adjusted that small things often bulked larger than big'. But in the perspective of the new world into which his paint and wig had got him it would be truer to say that everything, large and small, existed on an equality, and made up a fantastic republic. That world, being new, was not yet covered by the scales of custom and convention; the mind was free to consider every object in it. This ubiquity of interest is at the root of Sterne's humour, and nowhere more clearly than in the well-known incident of Uncle Toby and the fly.

'Go,' says he, one day at dinner, to an overgrown one which had buzzed about his nose, and tormented him cruelly all dinner time, and which, after infinite attempts, he had caught at last, as it flew past him:—'I'll not hurt thee,' says my Uncle Toby, rising from his chair, and going across the room with the fly in his hand, 'I'll not hurt a hair of thy head: Go,' says he, lifting up the sash, and opening his hand as he spoke, to let it escape, 'go, poor devil, get thee gone, why should I hurt thee? This world is surely wide enough to hold both thee and me.'

The force of this passage resides in its grasp of an unconventional relation between two living creatures; in a tender jogging of our minds, hardened by custom. Uncle Toby's action springs from an intuition of justice which only Sterne's mind could have discerned. There is this intellectual justification behind most of the passages which are blamed for their sentimentality or their licentiousness. What gives a peculiar fascination to these two qualities in his work, making them different from mere sentimentality and mere licentiousness, is that they spring from imaginative curiosity. The same insatiable intelligence which told him that asses and flies had their place, told him that the homunculus and the vital spirits had their place too; and what Thackeray called his 'latent corruption' was often the seeing of things in a novel perspective, the intuition that everything has its function and deserves its share of attention: homunculi and flies no less than asses and men.

It was Sterne's paint and wig and motley that got him into this world. What were the arts which he employed in it with such effect? They consisted of a few tricks as old as the vocation of the jester. The first was the pose of having so many difficulties to overcome that you cannot do what you want to do; another was that of having so much to tell that in following out this or that line you lose your way. The first was the favourite device of Grock; the second, that of Miss Bates in Jane Austen's *Emma*. Sterne rehearses over and over Grock's little act with the piano. First the piano is too far from the stool, so, with great labour, it has to be shifted; then the stool is too high, then too low; then one's feet cannot be accommodated; then some other unforeseen difficulty arises; but that is overcome too, for one is resolved to play. Sterne never gets to the stage of sitting down for long to his piece. With a great effort he does manage to get his hero born and misnamed; but then urgent interruptions crowd upon him; Tristram's parents, Tristram's uncle, the doctor who brought him into the world, the servants who assisted, have all to be attended to; for how is it possible to tell anything of Tristram if they are not disposed of first? But they are never disposed of; they are inexhaustible; and from them he is drawn aside by such things as noses, which also turn out to be inexhaustible. It is this inexhaustibility of things which calls Miss Bates into action. She suffers from an impossible discursiveness of interest. Everything that she mentions has the power of suggesting everything else; so that when she sets out to make one statement, she sets out to make every statement. Sterne checkmates her by a masterly employment of the parenthetic sentence, resulting in a series of Pyrrhic victories. So it goes on, with Grock peacefully and indefatigably obstructing the action, Miss Bates trying to say everything at once, and Sterne deploying his parenthetic sentence so well that she is checked perpetually on the frontier of incoherence.

From this description, Sterne's method seems the most impossible ever invented by a novelist. Yet it was out of the impossibilities that he snatched the triumphs of his art. All his divagations are short cuts. The struggle with insurmountable obstacles, the perpetual losing of the thread of the story to get everything in, are merely his devices for building up an image of the contradictoriness and variety of life. This image is produced not merely by what is said or what is told, but by the form of the work itself. Consequently he can as justly be called the most economical as the most wasteful of writers. Yet about his mastery of form there can be no doubt, for it is clear that he did exactly what he wanted to do, and one cannot imagine the pattern of his books as being other than it is; it may appear arbitrary, but it is inevitable.

Nevertheless it has a very peculiar kind of inevitability, the inevitability of a maze which while following the most exact laws of structure seems continuously to violate their purpose. *Tristram Shandy* is perhaps the only novel in the English language which is humorous in its construction, humorous, that is to say, through and through. And this means that what Sterne created was not merely a few comic figures inhabiting the world of ordinary fact, as Fielding and Scott and Dickens did, but a world of comic entities in which not merely his human figures, but everything from man down to the homunculus, are forms of humour. That world is as much a creation of poetic genius as the forest of Arden or the wood near Athens. And this is why Uncle Toby and Mr. Shandy have been so often called Shakespearean; they live like Falstaff and Bottom in a world of free comic entities, not in the world of actual knocks and blows, like Fielding's Partridge or Smollett's Commodore Truncheon. They are not figures of comedy in a picture of society, but naturals of humour in a world of universal forces.

BURNS AND POPULAR POETRY

FOR a Scotsman to see Burns simply as a poet is almost impossible. Burns is so deeply imbedded in Scottish life that he cannot be detached from it, from what is best and what is worst in it, and regarded as we regard Dunbar or James Hogg or Walter Scott. He is more a personage to us than a poet, more a figurehead than a personage, and more a myth than a figurehead. To those who have heard of Dunbar he is a figure, of course, comparable to Dunbar; but he is also a figure comparable to Prince Charlie, about whom everyone has heard. He is a myth evolved by the popular imagination, a communal poetic creation, a Protean figure; we can all shape him to our own likeness, for a myth is endlessly adaptable; so that to the respectable this secondary Burns is a decent man; to the Rabelaisian, bawdy; to the sentimentalist, sentimental; to the Socialist, a revolutionary; to the Nationalist, a patriot; to the religious, pious; to the self-made man, self-made; to the drinker, a drinker. He has the power of making any Scotsman, whether generous or canny, sentimental or prosaic, religious or profane, more wholeheartedly himself than he could have been without assistance; and in that way perhaps more human. He greases our wheels; we could not roll on our way so comfortably but for him; and it is impossible to judge impartially a convenient appliance to which we have grown accustomed.

The myth is unlike the man; but the man was its basis, and no other could have served. We cannot imagine

Wordsworth or Shelley or Tennyson or Shakespeare turning into a popular myth; and Burns did so because his qualities made it possible, and because he deserved it. No other writer has said so fully and expressly what every man of his race wanted him to say; no other writer, consequently, has been taken so completely into the life of a people. The myth may in some ways be absurd, but it is as solid as the agreement which rises in Scotsmen's minds whenever Burns utters one of his great platitudes:

> '*O wad some Pow'r the giftie gie us*
> *To see oursels as ithers see us!*'

> '*The hert aye's the part aye*
> *That makes us right or wrang.*'

> '*The best laid schemes o' mice and men*
> *Gang aft a-gley.*'

When the Burnsites are assembled on the Night, they feel Burns invisibly present among them as one of themselves, a great man who by some felicitous stroke has been transformed into an ordinary man, and is the greater because of it—a man indeed more really, more universally ordinary than any mere ordinary man could ever hope to be. This feeling is a tribute to Burns' humanity; it is a claim to kinship; it is also a grateful recognition that here is a poet for everybody, a poet who has such an insight into ordinary thoughts and feelings that he can catch them and give them poetic shape, as those who merely think or feel them cannot. This was Burns' supreme art. It appears to be simple. People are inclined to believe that it is easier to express ordinary thoughts and feelings in verse than complex and unusual ones. The problem is an artificial one, for in the end a poet does what he has a supreme gift for doing. Burns' gift lay there; it made him a myth; it predestined him to become the Rabbie of Burns Nights. When we consider Burns we must therefore include the Burns Nights with him, and the Burns cult in all its forms; if we sneer at them, we sneer at Burns. They are his reward, or his punishment (whichever the fastidious reader may prefer to call it) for having had the temerity to express the ordinary feelings of his people, and for having become a part of their life. What the Burns Nights ignore is the perfection of Burns' art, which makes him one of the great poets. But there is so much more involved that this, his real greatness, is scarcely taken into account.

Ordinary thoughts and feelings are not necessarily shallow, any more than subtle and unusual ones are necessarily profound. It may be said that Burns was never shallow and never profound. He did not have

Those thoughts that wander through eternity

which consoled Milton's Belial in Hell; and he could not be shallow as Tennyson sometimes was. He was sentimental, but sentimental with a certain solidity and grossness; there is genuine feeling behind his mawkishness, not merely a sick refinement of sensibility striving to generate the illusion of feeling. He could rise to the full height of the ordinary, where simplicity and greatness meet:

> *'Thou'll break my heart, thou bonie bird,*
> *That sings beside thy mate;*
> *For sae I sat, and sae I sang,*
> *And wist na o' my fate.'*

His rhetoric, his humour, his satire, his platitude have all the same solidity, the same devastating common sense. There is a great difference between *A Man's a Man for a' that* and

> *'Kind hearts are more than coronets,*
> *And simple faith than Norman blood.'*

60

The one speaks positively to us; the other says nothing. Burns became as amorphous as a myth because he was as solid as a ploughman. He became legendary because he was so startlingly ordinary. He was the ordinary man for whom Scotland had been looking as it might have looked for a king; and it discovered him with greater surprise and delight than if it had found a king, for kings are more common. His poetry embodied the obvious in its universal form, the obvious in its essence and its truth, the discovery of which is one of the perennial surprises of mankind. If Burns' poetry had not been obvious, he could never have become the national poet of Scotland.

But the national poet of Scotland is too conventional a term for him; the poet of the Scottish people is better, for all claim him. And by the people I do not mean merely the ploughman and the factory worker and the grocer's assist-ant, but the lawyer, the business man, the minister, the bailie—all that large class of Scotsmen who are not very interested in literature, not very cultivated, and know little poetry outside the poetry of Burns. It is these who have fashioned the popular image of Burns; and this is what really happens when a poet is taken into the life of a people. He moulds their thoughts and feelings; but they mould his too, sometimes long after he is dead. They make current a vulgarised image of him, and a vulgarised read-ing of his poetry; they take him into their life, but they also enter into his; and what emerges as the popular picture is a cross between the two. What is good in this bargain is self-evident—that the words and thoughts and feelings of a great poet become the common property of his people. The disadvantages I have tried to describe; they are natural and inevitable; compared to the single great advantage they do not matter very much, unless to those who cannot endure a normal dose of vulgarity. But they exist, and those who are advocating a more popular note in poetry at present should take them into account. For Burns is an object-lesson in what poetic popularity really means—the prime object-lesson in the poetry of the world, perhaps the unique instance.

It is good, then, that there should be 'poetry for the people', as its advocates call it. But there is another side of the question, and I found it illustrated while turning over an old number of the *Criterion* the other day, and coming on an editorial note by Mr. T. S. Eliot. A letter by the Poet Laureate and his friends had appeared in *The Times* under the heading, 'Art in the Inn'. Mr. Masefield proposed making use of the country public-house for 'verse-speaking, drama and readings of prose, and thus encouraging a wider appreciation of our language and literature in its highest forms'. Mr. Eliot was disconcerted by this proposal, as a number of us would be; for he 'had always thought of the public-house as one of the few places to which one could escape from verse-speaking, drama and readings of prose. If the public-house is to fall into the hands of the English Association and the British Drama League, where, one must ask bluntly, is a man to go for a drink?'

With this most people would agree; propaganda of this kind rests on a false basis; but Burns, at any rate, does not need it; when he is quoted or recited in pubs, the act is quite natural and spontaneous. But the more serious part of Mr. Eliot's comment comes later. 'I suspect that two distinct intentions, both laudable, have been confused. One is, that there should be a public for poetry. But what is important is not that this public should be large, but that it should be sensitive, critical and educated—conditions only possible for a small public. The other intention is, that people should be made happier, and be given the best life of which they are capable. I doubt whether poetry can be made to serve this purpose for the populace; if it ever does, it will never come as a result of centralised planning.'

Now, when Mr. Eliot doubts 'whether poetry can be made to serve this purpose' (of giving people the best life of which they are capable), he is evidently thinking of poetry as everyone who takes it seriously thinks of it; the poetry, to guess at his own tastes, of Dante, Shakespeare, Webster, Donne, Dryden, Baudelaire, the French Symbolists; but the list can be indefinitely extended, and for the genuine lover of poetry it will include Burns, shorn of his popularity, a name of the same kind as those other great names. If there is to be a public for these poets, and for what is good in the poetry of our own time, obviously Mr. Eliot is right in saying that it must be 'sensitive, critical and educated'; for without such a public poetry could not be preserved, and its traditions would be lost. Mr. Eliot asserts that this public is bound to be small, and no doubt that is so; but there is a fringe surrounding it which is not small, a working liaison between the discriminating few and the undiscriminating mass. Nothing can be done by propaganda or organisation to extend that fringe; but by merely existing it produces an effect among the mass which is different from the effect produced by popular poetry; for it is qualitative. What the advocates of poetry for the people should aim at is the dissemination of a feeling for quality, not the production of poetry which will be read in greater and greater quantity. This cannot be done by propaganda for popular poetry; but a beginning might be made by reform of our schools, where poetry is so often 'taught' in a way to make the pupil dislike it and misunderstand it.

Burns exists in both worlds—the world of quality and

the world of quantity. The world of quantity has grown so powerful and established such a firm hold on him that it is difficult to extricate him from its grip. He has certainly fulfilled one of the functions which Mr. Eliot doubted whether poetry could fulfil—'that people should be happier'; he has done much more than that; and what he has done is good beyond doubt, with this limitation which does not apply to other poets—that he has not brought poetry to people, but simply Burns. It may be that Burns is enough for many people who read him; but Shakespeare, or Milton, or Keats is not; to read one of them is to wish to read the others, and to discover poetry. Yet though Burns invisibly appears on Burns Nights, obedient to the summons, one feels that he too would have agreed with Mr. Eliot's opinion that the public for poetry should be 'sensitive, critical and educated'; for he knew something by experience which his admirers do not know —the desire for perfection and the endless pains of the artist.

WALTER SCOTT[1]

I SHOULD begin by expressing the sense of mingled honour and disadvantage which I feel in being asked to follow Sir Herbert Grierson as a lecturer on Scott. The honour I need not enlarge upon in this place; the disadvantage is equally obvious: for Sir Herbert is, I suppose, the chief authority on Scott now living, and I am only an admirer and periodical reader of that great novelist. Before preparing these lectures I re-read the two lectures which Sir Herbert gave a little more than four years ago. I was filled with admiration for the fine critical discrimination and the easy learning displayed in them, and the feeling they gave me that here someone was speaking who was a master of his subject. I cannot hope to emulate such a performance.

My own treatment of Scott will be much more tentative; I shall be concerned chiefly with some things in his character and work that puzzle and disconcert me. And first of all with a feeling I have often had after re-reading him. I experience the full shock of his imagination, but in a while I find it has left no lasting impression. Certain scenes and characters remain, along with a sense of abounding stir and bustle; but the full impact of a great mind, changing and illuminating one's apprehension of life, is not there. Or rather, after being present while I read, it is dissipated. In one of his lectures Sir Herbert Grierson quoted a contemporary of Scott as saying that he had not 'the gift of suggesting, as some poets can, by a few details far more than meets the eye, because they communicate

---

[1] The Walter Scott lecture for 1944, given at the University of Edinburgh

an emotional impression which of itself helps to evoke the complete picture'. The critic was speaking of Scott's poetry; but his observation applies also to the world of the Waverley Novels. They do not bring that quickening to the mind which sets the mind going by itself, as the work of lesser novelists such as Sterne and Thackeray and Jane Austen does. They do not go on working within us long after we have read them.

What reason can be found for this peculiarity of Scott's imagination? The most obvious one is a certain lack of intimacy. By universal testimony Scott was a frank and open-hearted man; but frankness has nothing to do with intimacy in this sense. Wordsworth was not frank, nor was Emily Brontë; yet both are intimate writers in a sense that Scott was not. For intimacy does not consist in a writer's telling us all about himself, but rather in communicating entire, with scrupulous fidelity, what his imagination reveals to him about life, whether it is pleasing or displeasing. Scott chose to keep something back; he lacked the overpowering compulsion. A writer who gives his imaginative vision entire must have a devotion to his work, the deliberate devotion of Wordsworth, or the instinctive devotion of Emily Brontë; and he must prize certain invisible things above the practical things of life. It is hard to judge whether Scott did this. He certainly was not devoted to his art as Wordsworth and Keats were, or even as Dickens and Thackeray were. The difficulty is to know to what he was chiefly devoted.

It has been said of Scott that he was too busy living to have much time or energy for writing. This is one of those absurd apologies which do him more harm than good. Yet we know that in his prime he liked to be ten hours a day outdoors, shooting, fishing or riding. John Buchan in his biography also insists that 'we shall not understand Scott unless we realise how much he lived in a secret world of his own, an inner world of dream and memory, from which he brought great treasures'. And a little later Buchan mentions quite a different side of him in saying that he 'liked the idea of marriage as a step in that progress in life to which one side of him was vowed'. The progress in life again, the getting-on, had to find some palpable symbol; that symbol was Abbotsford, a house which was equally suited to a great Border laird and a great Gothic novelist. Abbotsford in turn had to be kept up, and now and then enlarged; this involved the making of money on a great scale, and money could be made on a great scale only by writing rapidly one story after another. Finally even that was not sufficient; Scott needed money in still greater plenty, and without the necessary training or aptitude involved himself in a maze of business transactions. In this chaos of activities, his hunting and riding, his responsibilities as a country gentleman and a Border laird, his money-making, his writing, his social engagements in Edinburgh, his secret life of dream and memory, where did his main devotion lie? The question becomes still harder to answer when we reflect that two of the lives he led, his writing life, and his business life, he kept secret for many years. He was frank and open-hearted; but a frank and open-hearted man who keeps two of his lives secret, and cherishes in addition a secret world of his own of which even his published work shows few traces; a man of acknowledged good sense who squanders his health and finally his life to realise a fantastic dream—is a very difficult man to understand. Such riddles do not await our solution, but at most our respectful consideration; there can be no 'explanation' of Scott or of anyone else; if an explanation were forthcoming we should not know what to do with it; we should have to turn from it again to Scott himself.

But to establish within the circumference of the riddle some connections between Scott's character and his work should be possible. One of them is obvious enough. To writers of Scott's creative genius the practical activities in which they engage, however apparently irrelevant, are generally transformed into subject-matter for their imagination; even their errors and misfortunes are somehow turned to account. The same impulse which drove Scott to build Abbotsford enabled him to understand the man of ambition and the palpable form and bounds of a dream of earthly glory. Without his active hours in the open air he could not have described so convincingly men's enjoyment in exercising their physical powers. Even his business speculations must have helped him to realise by what curiously mixed ways the ambitious man achieves that respect and power which, seen from outside, appear to be quite without alloy.

In the discussion of *Hamlet* in Joyce's *Ulysses* the author makes John Eglinton say of Shakespeare's marriage to Anne Hathaway and his desertion of her afterwards, 'The world believes that Shakespeare made a mistake and got out of it as quickly and as best he could', to which Stephen Dedalus replies, 'Bosh! A man of genius makes no mistakes. His errors are volitional and are the portals of discovery.' This is the pure artist's point of view affirmed with fanatical conviction by a man who was resolved to put all his own mistakes into his work, and all the knowledge, pleasant and unpleasant, which they brought him. Scott's conception of his art was very different from Joyce's, and his estimation of his genius less arrogant; he accepted it and the delight it gave him, one imagines, very much as he accepted his delightful hours in the open air. Abbotsford no doubt became in time a portal of discovery; but it is certain that he did not regard it as such. And his mistakes, no matter how much he may have learned from them as a man and a novelist, remained mistakes in his eyes, whether volitional or not.

But whatever else went into his work, there was one episode in his life which never did so, or at best in the most shadowy and ghostlike way—his unsuccessful love affair as a young man with Williamina Stuart-Belsches, whose marriage to another suitor threw him into such despair that his friends were concerned for his life. We have evidence enough that his rejection by Williamina caused him lasting grief. While he was courting her he had cut her name on the turf beside the castle gate at St. Andrews. Thirty-four years later, sitting on an adjacent gravestone, he wondered why the name should still agitate his heart. A few months afterwards he met Lady Jane, Williamina's mother, in Edinburgh; Williamina had then been dead for seventeen years.

> I fairly softened myself like an old fool [he wrote], with recalling stories, till I was fit for nothing but shedding tears and repeating verses for the whole night. This is sad work. The very grave gives up its dead, and time rolls back thirty years to add to my perplexities.

After her marriage he had resolutely banished Williamina from his thoughts; but in spite of him she invaded his secret world, for it is said that on the eve of any great misfortune she appeared to him in his dreams.

In the summer after Williamina's marriage Scott's heart was 'handsomely pierced', as he put it, by a young lady whom he met during a visit to the English Lakes. Miss Charlotte Margaret Carpenter became his wife. Twelve years later he wrote to Lady Abercorn:

> Mrs. Scott's match and mine was of our own making, and proceeded from the most sincere affection on both sides, which has rather increased than diminished during twelve years'

marriage. But it was something short of love in all its forms, which I suspect people only feel once in all their lives; folk who have been nearly drowned in bathing rarely venturing a second time out of their depth.

Unlike Williamina, Mrs. Scott never entered his secret world.

This episode which Scott put so resolutely behind him but which refused to be banished altogether, filling him with agitation thirty years later when the object of his love was dead, making him prefer affection to love as a basis of marriage, was clearly one of the decisive experiences of his life. It is useless to speculate now what would have happened if Williamina had returned his love instead of rejecting it; yet one can hardly resist it. If he had married Williamina, would Abbotsford have become so important to him, would his ambition have fixed itself on such a limited and yet ostentatious object, would his ten hours a day in the open air have been so dear to him? And might not the development of his genius have been different, might not his imagination have acquired a greater intimacy from his experience of the most intimate of all human relations? In any case, the effect of her rejection of him was to make him turn away from one potentiality of experience for good. Yet as he was on one side a lover of adventure, like his heroes, the desire to venture out of his depth could not be eradicated so easily; he could not rid himself of it by marrying for affection instead of love. He had to venture out of his depth, and he did so in financial speculation. It was in business that he indulged his need for adventure.

A natural reticence in Scott, confirmed by the literary and moral conventions of his time, prevented him from re-creating in imagination the story of his early love. Or perhaps the memory was so painful that he could not bear to recall it. John Buchan praises him for this abstention, but it seems to be a matter neither for praise nor for blame; we do not blame Shakespeare for his sonnets. Scott was not devoted to the art of writing with the fanaticism of a modern novelist like Joyce, nor prepared to offer up to it his buried secrets. Nevertheless it is possible that Joyce's generalisation has a certain point if we apply it to Scott's resolve to put the memory of Williamina behind him; for that was probably the main reason for his inability to portray love, and for the great number of insipid female figures in his novels. His old women, his peasant women, his queens and princesses, his gipsies and vagabonds, all of them by virtue of age or class unlikely to prove dangerous to any of the young heroes in whom we see an image of Scott himself at the stage when he was in love with Williamina, are drawn with a sure hand. The others, the potentially dangerous ones, seem to fall in love because in a romance they are expected to do so; and their love stories would quickly weary us, and Scott too, if they were not enlivened with all sorts of intrigues and dangers.

It seems plausible to think, then, that the disastrous outcome of Scott's affair with Williamina and the resolution with which he put her memory behind him contracted the scope of his imagination and made it impossible for him to describe love. It may have been, too, the cause of his general lack of intimacy. For some reason he could not say the most intimate thing of all, the thing which might have given him the gift 'of suggesting by a few details far more than meets the eye, because they communicate an emotional impression which of itself helps to evoke the completer picture'. The emotional impression is lacking. He would always have been one of the great objective writers. But if the course of his life had been different, he might have conveyed in his picture of life a more profound sense of significance. The bustle, the energy, the humour and pathos of life are there as they are nowhere else, even in Balzac and Tolstoy; but there is no serious criticism of life. When Scott expresses a judgment of experience it comes from the secret world where the memory of Williamina was buried, and its burden is that all is vanity, the bustle, the adventure, the glory, everything that he created with such genial warmth and abundance:

> *Look not thou on beauty's charming,*
> *Sit thou still when kings are arming. . . .*
> *Stop thine ear against the singer,*
> *From the red gold keep thy finger—*
> *Vacant heart, and hand, and eye,*
> *Easy live and quiet die.*

If we are conscious of an emptiness beneath the bustle and action of his novels, and beneath the surface of his busy life, the reason may lie here.

The affair with Williamina may possibly throw some light on another trait of Scott—his grossly practical attitude to his writings, which is like that of a man who turns from a high satisfaction to make sure of a lower one. In the introductory epistle to *The Fortunes of Nigel* he speaks very frankly:

> No one shall find me rowing against the stream. I care not who knows it—I write for general amusement. . . . A man should strike when the iron is hot, and hoist sail while the wind is fair. If a successful author keeps not the stage, another instantly takes his ground.

If we accept this statement, we shall be forced to think that Scott had no aim but success. Yet 'I care not who knows it' implies at least that he was not proud of what he was saying. And he softens the effect of his declaration later by a more plausible explanation of his hurried and careless method of composition:

I should be chin-deep in the grave, man, before I had done with my task, and in the meanwhile, all the quirks and quiddities which I might have devised for my readers' amusement would lie rotting in my gizzard.

The creations of his imagination crowded in upon him so thick and fast that he had to deal with them as best he could.

Yet there was a genuine reason for his determination to keep the stage and not resign it to the next comer; for he was always in need of money, since he was driven by another impulse just as powerful as his imagination, the ambition whose symbol was Abbotsford. Ambition on a large scale generally involves the taking of risks. He himself was adventurous on one side and prudent on another, as befitted the son of an impulsive and imaginative mother and a respectable and practical father. In his life these two sides of him seem to have played a complicated game of hide-and-seek with each other. As a writer he lived in a secret world of romance and adventure, while to his acquaintances he existed as a respectable gentleman of means. The curious thing is that it was the romancer and adventurer who produced the means, and the respectable gentleman who squandered them. One does not know whether to regard Abbotsford as the dream of the romancer, or the final justification of the man of position. There is a stage in Scott's life after which it is almost impossible to disentangle his business and social from his literary activities, for they fall into the position of cause and effect, the income from his novels paying his debts, and the dream of Abbotsford forcing him to get still more deeply into debt. The romantic world he created in his books became a sort of bank from which he drew the credit to realise the ideal of a splendid traditional Border community with himself at its head. If he had succeeded in realising that ideal it would probably have satisfied both sides of him, the romantic and the social.

In this confusion of activities which makes up Scott's life as a man, where each activity seems to be performing a function better suited to the others, where writing is regarded as a means of making money and business turns out to be a means of losing it, we are brought up once more against his regardless attitude to his genius. His genius and his ambition pulled him in opposite directions. His ambition was not to be known as a great writer, but to achieve a distinguished position in society and to live a life of traditional grandeur in the Border country and of social influence in Edinburgh. Wordsworth did not know that division, nor on a different level did Dickens; their genius and their ambition were set in the same direction; they put all of themselves into their work; they had no Abbotsford.

There remains Scott's secret world into which Williamina found her way, and no one else so far as we know. When he draws upon it its message is unmistakable and tells us that all action is vain, as in Lucy's song in *The Bride of Lammermoor*, or predetermined by necessity, as in Redgauntlet's outburst on liberty of choice. It is concerned with death and the grave, as in *Proud Maisie* and the conversation between the old women in the churchyard when the Master of Ravenswood rides away. These are the voices of his secret world. Is it fanciful to imagine that they bring us back again to Williamina Stuart-Belsches, who still existed in his secret world although she was dead, and was twice dead to him through her first rejection of him? Among the novels, there is most of his secret world in *The Bride of Lammermoor*, which he wrote in a delirium of pain, so that he could not remember a single scene when it was shown to him, and found the whole 'monstrous, gross and grotesque'. In some of his later novels there is evidence that he had accepted consciously its pessimistic reading of life, his physical powers and his vast capacity for enjoyment having by then declined. There is the passage towards the end of *Woodstock*:

> Years rush by us like the wind. We see not whence the eddy comes, nor whitherward it is tending, and we seem ourselves to witness their flight without a sense that we are changed; and yet Time is beguiling man of his strength as the wind robs the woods of their foliage.

There is Redgauntlet's outburst on free-will:

> The privilege of free action belongs to no mortal—we are tied down by the fetters of duty—our mortal path is limited by the regulations of honour—our most indifferent actions are meshes of the web of destiny by which we are all surrounded. . . . Yes, young man, in doing and suffering we play but the part allotted to us by Destiny, the manager of this strange drama—stand bound to act no more than is prescribed, to say no more than is set down for us; and yet we mouth about free-will, and freedom of thought and action, as if Richard must not die, or Richmond conquer, exactly where the Author has decreed it shall be so.

This is the comment of Scott's secret world on the world of bustling action. What gives *Redgauntlet* a unique place among the Waverley Novels is that it shows us a man of action aware of the vanity of action, who continues the fight in spite of that knowledge, 'tied down by the fetters of duty', 'limited by the regulations of honour'. Compared with him Scott's other heroes live in a world of illusion. Their world is more rich and various and coloured and in a sense more full of interest than Redgauntlet's predetermined world. It is the world which Scott most enjoyed describing; but to one who knew Redgauntlet's world and who wrote, 'life could not be endured were it seen in its reality', it must sometimes have appeared to be a world suspended over nothingness.

II

The imperfections of a great writer are like the flaws in a precious stone; they should be regarded as qualities rather than faults. In Scott's case we have to take into account an attribute of the precious stone distinct from its quality or its rarity—its size. His mere bulk adds something spectacular and stupendous to him which his contemporaries felt and we can still feel. Where all is so huge, the faults are huge too; they are so obvious that certain critics have never been able to see beyond them. Mr. E. M. Forster, a man of genius and intelligence, has said that Scott is not even a good story-teller, and has demonstrated it by an amusing account of the plot of *The Antiquary*.

Scott was a very great story-teller, as well as a very bad one. *The Antiquary* certainly contains one of his worst plots. But his particular kind of story-telling did not depend on plot, and was often good in spite of it, the story being excellent even where the plot was mediocre or bad. A coherent plot obviously adds greatly to the total effect of a story, since in it all the incidents contribute to that effect. Such a story stays in the memory, not as a collection of episodes, but as a whole, and the cumulative movement of the action produces that emotional impression, the absence of which from Scott's poetry has been mentioned. This concentrated effect, which is like the effect of a whole mind directed on a single object, we find seldom in Scott's novels, and perhaps only in two—*The Heart of Midlothian*, his greatest story, and *The Bride of Lammermoor*, the story in which we have the strongest impression of fate.

But the coherent necessitated plot is not his typical plot. His art as a story-teller could not have expanded to its

76

full freedom within it, for with its emphasis on unity it did not give scope for the enormous degree of variety which he claimed. His stories in general have a direction; they set out from one point to reach another; but they take a rambling course, and there is nothing which they may not gather in before they reach their end. All the events in a story like *The Bride of Lammermoor* carry the mind forward to the conclusion. But in most of the Waverley Novels our minds are immediately fascinated by the succession of changing scenes which the journey produces, and the end is disappointing, being merely a conventional end. These stories consist mostly of middle; their abundance is all packed between the two conventions without which a story cannot exist, since it must start somehow and end somehow. The freedom which Scott demands from his plot, once he has started from some-where to reach somewhere, is really a freedom to explore the whole human scene; and the laboured complication of the action is only a means to evoke a sense of the natural complication of human life. He is never tired of involving his plots, but he does so because he is endlessly interested in character and situation. And how brilliantly he manages it; his skill puts him among the greatest story-tellers.

The Fortunes of Nigel contains one of his most compli-cated plots. By any standard it is far too involved; the sequence of accidents to the papers securing young Lord Glenvarlich's possession of his estates becomes monstrous, absurd, almost wearisome. But what a variety of characters and scenes are gathered into the story by this stratagem, and what a liveliness is communicated to them by the vigour of the action. We must accept the complication of these plots as an artificial but necessary convention, as we accept the convention of romantic opera.

In *The Fortunes of Nigel* Scott states a whole series of

themes; the historical novelty of life in seventeenth-century London, the hostility between the English and the Scots whom the King had drawn south along with him, the connection with the mob through Vincent the apprentice, the connection with the Court through George Heriot. All this is stated in the first few chapters, and in the succeeding ones the fabric grows until it takes in the whole life of London. If Balzac had concentrated his powers to fill such a canvas, he would have done it in sections, devoting a separate book to each. Scott gathers the endless variety into one colossal whole. He does this without falling into confusion. The characters are thrown together pell-mell in the action; the classes intermingle in all sorts of ways; yet each figure remains as firmly in his station as the characters in the Prologue to *The Canterbury Tales*. Only a writer with Scott's fine sense of proportion could have been both so involved and so orderly. But the involution was necessary; it was the only means by which a novelist of action could have given an impression of the complication of human life.

The Fortunes of Nigel is Scott's most baroque work. *Old Mortality* is comparatively simple because there he had a historical subject, the religious struggle in Scotland in the second half of the seventeenth century: the murder of Archbishop Sharpe and the battles of Drumclog and Bothwell Brig play an essential part in it. The action had to be woven round these important happenings. The invention is not free, therefore, as in *The Fortunes of Nigel*, being used to show in what ways the creed of the extreme Covenanters affected their character and speech, and above all to state dramatically the case of the two sides to the dispute. Members of the opposing parties get entangled in personal relations with one another, as in *The Fortunes of Nigel*, their humanity prevailing over their opinions and loyalties.

This happens in all the novels. Scott keeps two things evenly balanced: his sense of universal humanity, and his awareness of the conventions of society. The first enables him to let people of all classes intermingle; the second, to keep them intact in their places. No other novelist does this so surely. We may object to the philosophy of life implied by this performance, which is that of a traditional Tory; we may object to its being done at all; but we cannot but admire the perfection with which it is done. One might almost say that Scott puts man in his place, or rather in what was once his place. And he does it so perfectly because he does it absent-mindedly.

In *Old Mortality* Scott needed all his objectivity, for he was dealing with an issue which was alive in his time and is not yet dead. Mr. Forster complains that Scott lacks both imaginative passion and artistic detachment. Actually Scott's detachment is sometimes disconcerting, is pushed to an extreme where we feel that nothing matters. It comes too easily; we feel he has no right to it. But in *Old Mortality* he had to make a hard effort to achieve detachment and state the case for both sides fairly, and this gives a tension to the action which is absent from most of the other novels.

But Scott's story-telling was, of course, mainly a device for delineating character. His most obvious virtue as a painter of character is the complexity of impression he achieves by apparently simple means. We tend to think of his characters as simple characters; yet if we examine them we discover that hardly one is simple. Compared with those of Dickens or Fielding or Thackeray, they have infinite light and shade; though the light is so exactly where it should be, and the shadow falls so naturally, that we scarcely notice it. Yet they are all complex and surprising: Bailie Nicol Jarvie with his mixture of business sharpness and love of adventure; Andrew Fairservice with his cunning, conceit, self-righteousness and rustic poetry; and above all, James the Sixth of Scotland and First of England. Scott never tells us what James is thinking; he reveals him entirely through what he does and says. Yet he gives as completely as anyone could an impression of the bottomless complexity of that curious man, and leaves him a rounded character, a human being who successfully reconciles within himself outrageous irreconcilables. We cannot observe how it is done, the use of light and shade is so fine, yet the figure so definite. Thackeray lavished all his skill on Becky Sharp, but she seems laboured and crude compared even with Scott's minor characters.

His supreme means for the revelation of character is of course dialogue; one feels sometimes that the action is contrived simply to give the characters an opportunity to speak out. And they put all of themselves into what they say, their dispositions, their moods, their memories, their philosophies. Scott knew that his main strength lay here, as he shows in an ironical imaginary dialogue between Dick Tinto, a painter, and himself at the beginning of *The Bride of Lammermoor*. 'Your characters', Dick tells him, 'make too much use of the *gob box*; they *patter* too much; there is nothing in whole pages but mere chat and dialogue.' The author replies: 'The ancient philosopher was wont to say, "speak, that I may know thee"; and how is it possible for an author to introduce his *personae dramatis* to his readers in a more interesting and effectual manner than by the dialogue in which each is represented as supporting his own appropriate character?'

Scott's persons support their appropriate characters with unexampled eloquence, yet with the most exact proportion. Mr. Forster once remarked that the whole of Mrs. Micawber could be summed up in the sentence: 'I shall never desert Mr. Micawber'. Scott's characters cannot be contained in such formulas. They are not made up of one or two set qualities like the characters of Dickens; we feel that they are moulded from the substance of which human life is made, and contain all or almost all its attributes, the only difference between one character and another being that these attributes are compounded in different proportions. So that beyond the individual compounding there is something universally human which may burst out in some emergency, as in Jeanie Deans' appeal to the Queen.

In their light and shade and something unexpected in them, Scott's characters are unlike those of any other Scottish or English writer except some of Sterne's; for Sterne too was fascinated by the complexity of human nature. They are more like the characters of a novelist who in every other way was as unlike Scott as possible—Dostoevsky, particularly in the superb comic vein which he displays in the first part of *The Possessed*. Scott's characters have greater wholeness and harmony, and Dostoevsky's greater depth; but there is in both the same ability to be alive in a surprising way, as long as they are on the stage. Scott's grasp of the complexity of character came from his perception of human wholeness, and Dostoevsky's from his knowledge of man's inward division. But in their management of light and shade and a certain concealed or implied wit, they strikingly resemble each other.

Scott and Dostoevsky resemble each other in another way too, in their power to make their characters now and then say things of more than individual significance and turn them into voices which seem to speak for whole classes of humanity to all humanity. The best way to give an idea of these utterances is to quote some of them:

I have had mony a thought, that whan I faund mysell auld and forfairn, and no able to enjoy God's blessed air ony langer, I wad drag mysell here wi' a pickle aitmeal—and see, there's a bit bonny drapping well that popples that selfsame gate simmer and winter—and I wad e'en streck mysell out here, and abide my removal, like an auld dog that trails his useless ugsome carcase into some bush or bracken, no to gie living things a scunner wi' the sight o't when it's dead—Ay, and then, when the dogs barked at the lone farmstead, the gudewife wad cry, "Whisht, stirra, that'll be auld Edie," and the bits o' weans wad up, puir things, and toddle to the door, to pu' in the auld Blue Gown that mends a' their bonny-dies—but there wad be nae word mair o' Edie, I trow.'

'I have been flitting every term these four and twenty years; but when the time comes there's aye something to saw that I would like to see sawn—or something to maw that I would like to see mawn—or something to ripe that I would like to see ripen—and sae I e'en daiker on wi' the family frae year's end to year's end. . . . But if your honour wad wush me ony place where I wad hear pure doctrine, and hae a free cow's grass, and a cot, and a yard, and mair than ten punds of annual fee, and where there was nae leddy about the town to count the apples, I'se hold mysell muckle indebted to ye.'

'It's weel wi' you gentles, that can sit in the house wi' hand-kerchers to your een when ye lose a friend; but the likes o' us maun to our wark again if our hearts were beating as hard as my hammer. There's a curse either on me or on this auld black bitch of a boat that I have hauled high and dry and patched and clouted sae mony years, that she might drown my poor Steenie at the end of them, and be d—d to her! Yet what needs ane be angry at her, that has neither soul nor sense? though I am no that muckle better mysell. She's but a rickle o' auld rotten deals, warped wi' the wind and the sea—and I am a dour carle, battered by foul weather at sea and land till I am maist as senseless as hersell. She maun be mended though again' the morning tide—that's a thing o' necessity.'

'Do you see that blackit and broken end of a shealing?—There my kettle boiled for forty years—there I bore twelve buirdly sons and daughters—Where are they now?—Where are the leaves that were on that auld ash-tree at Martinmas! the

west wind has made it bare—and I'm stripped too.—Do you see
that saugh-tree?—it's but a blackened rotten stump now—I've
sat under it mony a bonny summer afternoon, when it hung its
gay garlands ower the poppling water—I've sat there and I've
held you on my knee, Henry Bertram, and sung ye sangs of the
auld barons and their bloody wars—It will ne'er be green again,
and Meg Merrilies will never sing sangs mair, be they blithe or
sad. But ye'll no forget her?—and ye'll gar big up the auld wa's
for her sake? and let somebody live there that's ower gude to fear
them of another world—For if ever the dead come back among
the living, I'll be seen in this glen mony a night after these
crazed banes are in the mould.'

In passages like these Scott speaks simultaneously from
his daylight and his secret world.

II

FRIEDRICH HÖLDERLIN

HÖLDERLIN is a difficult poet to understand, not because his language is particularly obscure, but because the world of his imagination is arranged in such an unusual way. From the first his mind was possessed by the classical world, and Greece in particular, with its gods and its elements, fire, water, air, the ether. He lived in that world more exclusively than any other modern poet has done. Then came his mental breakdown: grief for the loss of Susette Gontard shattered his mind, smashing his classical world to pieces; but the pieces survived, though the connecting structure was damaged; and in the later poems we find these fragments appearing in a new order.

To look for ordinary logic in that order would be useless. Yet it is more significant than the first, normal, order; for it is immediately related to an intense personal experience. *Der Archipelagus* is a magnificent reconstruction of ancient Greece; but it is cold compared with a poem like *Patmos*, in which Hercules, John the Baptist, the disciples, Christ, Henry IV at Canossa seem to come as close to Hölderlin, though in fits and starts, as the contortions of his own grief. Experience transformed his classical world from an imaginative picture into a kind of mythology.

His poetry had always been symbolical in a definite sense; when he wrote a poem on the oak, for instance, he did not mean any oak that could be seen by the eye, but an idea. The palpable world was impalpable to him, and ideas palpable: one has only to turn to the titles of some of his poems: 'Der Mensch', 'Des Morgens', 'Die Götter', 'Der Frieden', 'An die Hoffnung', 'An den Frühling', 'Die Liebe', and compare the conventional themes with his treatment of them. But in the poems which he wrote after his breakdown this symbolism became more significant, for it expressed his immediate experience and therefore speaks, though in a curious language, to ours.

This language is curious in two ways: it is highly personal; and it is disconnected with the significant disconnectedness of dreams. To take the first quality: when Hölderlin speaks of Bacchus, Hercules, the gods in general, the elements, love, poetry, home, country, man, he means something personal and at the same time constant and unchanging. Rilke in the *Duinese Elegies* attaches a private meaning to the Angels; and Yeats, if we are to accept *A Vision* as a handbook to his poems, attaches a private meaning to everything. But these private meanings of Rilke and Yeats have nothing in common with Hölderlin's meanings, which seem to arise as a direct response to a vision. Rilke tried to explain the meaning of his Angels, and Yeats has explained the whole system of thought which provided his poetry with metaphors. But the specific meanings which Hölderlin attributes to certain entities seems to be inherent in his mere grammatical use of them, to be implied in the manner in which, as words, they come into a sentence. These particular terms are like fragments of a different kind of speech, simple, inexplicable, constant, incapable of being replaced by any rational explanation of them. Hercules is always Hercules, stationary, timeless, and it is the same with the other entities to which Hölderlin ascribes this peculiar significance. As these entities are constant elements in his later poetry, they give it, as well as this baffling depth, a certain radiant monotony. Most of his later poems are very like one another.

The disconnectedness of his poetry is related to his peculiar use of words as well as to his madness; or rather they go together. In the words representing Bacchus, Hercules, the gods, the home as a static pattern, we have an explanation of the abrupt transitions which fill his poetry, the recurring effect of passing at one step from the world of time and change to that of timelessness, and back again. The contrast between change and changelessness impressed him early, and found its perfect expression in *Schickalslied*, where the gods are described as wandering in light, fateless, their eyes gazing in still, eternal clarity, and men as stumbling and falling every moment like water flung from cliff to cliff.

After Hölderlin's madness these two worlds became confused in his mind, and his language took on simultaneously a new fullness and obscurity. The fullness cannot be separated from the obscurity; or rather it is one of its causes. For the obscurity springs mainly from the fact that certain words seem to carry more meaning than they can hold; their meaning is too big for them, and produces a sense of something vast but confused. Analysis or rationalisation of them can therefore do very little with them. It is the same with certain statements in his poems, quite simple in appearance; for example, where he says in *Patmos* in the middle of the description of Asia rising with its thousand fragrant peaks,

> *And blinded I sought*
> *Something I knew,*

which in the original is so densely charged with mystery. There are other statements which become strange because 'and' is used where one would expect 'but'; it is as if Hölderlin's imagination were so full that he had to use the uniting conjunction instead of the qualifying one:

Near is the god
And hard to grasp.

The unique rearrangement of his shattered world is partly responsible, doubtless, for such conjunctions, since the gods and the elements live there on the same plane as mankind, and there is no hard and fast barrier between time and eternity; so that what would appear a qualification or a contradiction in an ordinary statement is in Hölderlin's world the self-evident continuation of a simple assertion. That is, if we can call what Hölderlin created a world. It is rather a radiant chaos, containing fragments of a world which has been some time or will be some time, where there are more freely co-existing elements than can be compressed into the ordinary world, or have yet been compressed into it; and these by their mere presence suggest a whole which, as there is nowhere else to put it, evokes the thought of some distant future. Hölderlin is particularly equivocal in his treatment of time; it is sometimes hard to tell whether he is writing about the past or the future, or an unchanging present. And because this brings the present and the past together, evoking a possibility of a new mode of perception, it suggests the future.

To speculate upon what Hölderlin's poetry owed to his mental instability is useless, for as soon as we set down one of the qualities of his poetry to derangement, we discover that it can be interpreted as something else. His confusion of past and present, the gods and men, the timeless and the transitory, is perhaps an effect of mental disturbance; but it has another aspect in which that confusion seems to come from a more than usually concrete grasp of certain truths: that the past exists in the present, that the gods (or what Hölderlin meant by them) mingle with human history, that time and timelessness are inextricably bound up. All this can be read into his poetry, not as ideas clothed in images, but as a direct and simple recognition. Ideas were concrete presences to him, and that is one of the main causes of the strangeness of his poetry: reduce these presences back to ideas again—they can never be completely reduced—and there is nothing mad, nothing even extraordinary about them.

The derangement of Hölderlin's mind can be more clearly seen in the extreme disconnectedness of some of his poetry, where a gap seems to yawn between one statement and the next, producing an effect as if the reader closed his eyes for a moment and found himself in a different place when he opened them again. Yet even this can produce superb results, as in the passage in *Patmos* which follows Hölderlin's announcement that he intends to sing of Christ as he had sung of Hercules:

> *Immeasurable*
> *The fable since Him. And now*
> *I would sing the journey of the nobles*
> *To Jerusalem, and anguish wandering in Canossa,*
> *And Henry. Except courage itself*
> *Fail me. That must*
> *Be taken into account. For like morning mist are*
> *the names*
> *Since Christ. Become dreams. Fall like error.*
> *On the heart, and deadly if no one*
> *Ponder what they are and understand.*

The real demoralisation of Hölderlin's mind can be seen rather in some of his very last poems, which are free from any touch of strangeness, completely personal, and move us not as poetry, but as an intimate expression of his long-continued suffering:

FRIEDRICH HÖLDERLIN

Das Angenehme dieser Welt hab ich genossen.
Der Jugend Freuden sind wie lang! wie lang! verflossen.
April und Mai und Junius sind ferne.
Ich bin nichts mehr, ich lebe nicht mehr gerne.

'I have enjoyed the pleasant things of this world. The joys of youth have faded long, long ago. April and May and June are far away. I am nothing now, I no longer wish to live.' That is moving when we know who wrote it; but as poetry, except for the beautiful third line, it has little more than a specialised interest. We feel that when Hölderlin wrote these lines the world in which his imagination had lived was not only in ruins but vanished without a trace, leaving merely the carpenter's house in Tübingen and his daily round.

The imagination in Hölderlin's poetry is obviously related to dreams. It is not the kind of imagination which deals with ordinary experience—for instance, the life around it—but has its subject-matter given to it in a quite different way, somewhat as the subject-matter of a dream is given in sleep. It has therefore very little specifically to do with the contemporary world, like a good deal of romantic poetry and almost all mystical poetry. Or at most it regards the contemporary world as the Old Testament prophets regarded it: that is, in general terms, as falling short of its vision. This imagination is unlike any other kind; for while it works with greater freedom than ordinary imagination, one can hardly say on what it works: the ancestral racial dream material of which Jung speaks, or the delusive desires of mankind in all ages. It is related to prophecy (Isaiah) on the one hand, and to dream literature (De Quincey) on the other. The real assumption of this kind of poetry is that human existence can be changed, or rather will be changed; just as the assumption of dramatic poetry is that human existence is unchangeable. There seems to be no compromise between these two views.

HÖLDERLIN'S *PATMOS*

THERE are three separate versions of *Patmos*, the first two complete, the third fragmentary. The second very closely follows the first and is an improved version of it. The third, which is considerably more obscure, contains several alterations and additions. The subject of the poem is not St. John, as the title might indicate, but Christ; and it marks a turning point in Hölderlin's imaginative interpretation of history and time, for which in his earlier poetry Greece and the gods of Greece had stood as the supreme symbols. He seems to have begun the poem with the intention of including Christ in this personal hierarchy. The attempt failed, as he confesses in the course of the third version:

> *John. Christ. These I would sing*
> *As I have sung Hercules. . . .*
> > *But that*
> *Cannot be. A destiny is different. More marvellous*
> *To sing, richer.*

That is his indirect and almost bemused confession that Christ could not be included among the other gods. The problem had touched him in an earlier poem, *Der Einzige*. 'I have seen many beautiful things,' he says, 'and I have sung God's image that lives among men. . . . But when I enquired among the ancients, the heroes and the gods, why did You stay away?' Trying to pick up his former style he goes on to compare Christ with Bacchus, but then says: 'Yet a feeling of shame hinders me from likening You with men of this world', by which, in spite of the

92

strangeness of the designation, Bacchus was obviously meant. He continues: 'And I know that he who bore You, your Father, the same who—'. Then comes a blank line, followed by: 'For never does He rule alone'. The poem shows throughout an intense vacillation of mind, which culminates in that missing line. It is an involuntary confession, retracted and given again, for he goes on: 'But on One hangs my love. This time the song has come too straight from my heart; yet I will make good the error in my next one, if I ever sing another. Never can I strike the balance as I would wish.' The balance in general; perhaps also the balance between the gods and Christ. This problem was clearly one which troubled Hölderlin during those years, and in *Patmos* it finds its most complete resolution.

Before considering *Patmos* itself it might be best to say something of the poetry of Hölderlin's later period of which it is the crown. That poetry draws part of its inspiration from history, and shows, though in a rudimentary form, an understanding of what we call the historical sense. Hölderlin as a young man was a friend of Hegel and Schelling; they read Plato, Kant and Jacobi together; and he was influenced by their ideas. But in the essence of his genius and in his attitude to what he regarded as the chief problem of existence—the ways by which God makes himself known to man—he was nearer to Wordsworth than to any other writer. Like Wordsworth, he was concerned with Man, not with the men of his own or any particular civilisation or age. But while Wordsworth found God in nature, Hölderlin found Him in history, in time. To divine the workings of God in history is what we call prophecy. The prophet in the narrower sense foresees these workings in the future: Hölderlin saw them in the past as well, in the universal story of mankind. It is this perception that gives the prophetic part of his poetry its unique intonation, as of a single voice speaking to the gods in a solitude. His utterance is like that of a man accounting to himself for things which he cannot tell to others. The impression of vastness produced by his poetry is due to the fact that the past with all its powers—gods, heroes, emanations—was as real to him as the present. The past was not something that could be thrown into contrast, or paralleled, with the present, as in the poetry of Mr. Eliot and Mr. Pound. It widened the present in a striking and incalculable way; and this expansion gives us a sense of a vast whole, a universal dispensation which is the life of mankind from beginning to end. As all prophecy looks to the fulfilment of time, this vastness is a normal element in prophetic writing, and is the source of its vagueness and grandeur. Hölderlin's prophetic inspiration determined also the metre and the rhythm of his later poetry. The poetry of his first period is written in regular measure of various kinds, including rhymed verse, hexameters, alcaics and sapphics. His prophetic poetry is in a sort of free rhythm.

Patmos is a long poem; in parts its meaning is extremely obscure; the punctuation throughout is peculiar and deliberately so, and the poetic period, the sentence, is ample far beyond the usual limit of German poetry, often being carried forward, with a deliberate effect of bridging great spaces, from one strophe to the next. I have not attempted to render the whole poem, but have made excerpts long enough to give, as far as that can be done in a verse rendering, an idea of its style and its argument. Where obscurity exists I have not tried to clarify it. The poem begins:

> *Near is God*
> *And hard to seize.*
> *But where danger is, there*
> *Rises the saviour also.*

In darkness dwell
The eagles, and fearless go
The sons of the mountains over the abyss
On light bridges.
Therefore since round are piled
The peaks of Time, and the best beloved
Dwell near at hand, languishing
On inaccessible hills,
O give us innocent water,
Wings give us, that with steady hearts
We may go thither and return again.

This is the introduction, which is in the nature of an invocation. I have done my best to give an idea of the rhythm of the verse, but there is no way of reproducing in English the peculiarly condensed style, which can be seen in the first two lines:

Nah ist
Und schwer zu fassen der Gott.

Nor have I been able to render the indefiniteness of such expressions as 'der Gott', which may be understood in its context either as 'God' or 'the god', or of 'das Rettende', which does not mean so much the saviour as 'that which saves', or perhaps by a stretch of association the saving grace. The images in this verse are all vast and shadowy, and they are assembled in an ordered confusion which is intensified by such juxtapositions as that of the beloved dwelling near at hand and languishing on inaccessible hills. This omission of connecting links is characteristic of the poem, and of the kind of poetry to which it belongs, where mystery is not a thing to be explained, but an indefeasible presence.

After this beginning the poem continues:

So I spoke, then a genius led me
More swiftly than I could tell from my house,
And far, whither I never

Thought to come. Darkened
In twilight as I went
The shadowy forest
And the longing brooks
Of home; never had I seen these lands;
But soon in first-born splendour,
Mysterious
In golden smoke,
Swiftly awakened
Under the tread of the sun
With a thousand fragrant peaks

Asia bloomed, and blinded I sought
Something I knew, for strange to me
The broad lanes where down
From Tmolus journeyed
Gold-hemmed Pactolus,
And Taurus stood and Messogis,
And full of flowers the gardens,
A still fire. But in the light
Bloomed high the silvery snow,
And sign of immortal life,
On inaccessible walls
Ancient the ivy grew, and there were upborne
On living pillars, cedars and laurels,
The solemn,
The divinely-built palaces.

This is a vision of the ancient world to which Hölderlin turned for relief. The extraordinary length of the chief period and its continuation into the next verse convey a sense of dreamlike swiftness of movement through vast distances of time and space. The carrying of these great periods over from one verse to another, spanning the gap which he deliberately leaves between them, and thus lengthening still more, by the introduction of an unknown dimension, the stretch of his flying imagination, is a device peculiar to Hölderlin in his time. In the original the movement of this passage is noble and mysterious.

The second version continues from here:

> *But round Asia's portals*
> *In the precarious wilderness of sea*
> *There are shadowless ways enough*
> *Leading this way and that,*
> *Yet the isles are known to the sailor.*

This is his prelude to his first mention of Patmos, but he must have felt later that it was inadequate, for he altered it in his fragmentary third version. After

> *And full of flowers the gardens,*

which he changed to,

> *And almost sleepy with flowers the gardens,*

he leaves a blank and continues, abruptly changing the scene from Greece to Judaea:

> *The airs of Jordan and Nazareth*
> *And of Capernaum far from the sea*
> *And of Galilee and Cana.*
> *For a little while I shall be with you, he said. With*
> *   such drops*
> *He stilled the sighing of the light, the thirsty wilderness*
> *Was as in the days when through all Syria*
> *The slaughtered children wept*
> *Still gracious in death, and the plucked head*
> *Of the Baptist was like unfading script*
> *Visible on the unscathed dish. Like fire*
> *Are the voices of God.*

Here the images are extraordinarily vivid but confused, seeming inextricably to mingle the past and the present, or to set them side by side in some new order. Two separate aspects of time appear to be fused in the lines

> *and the plucked head*
> *Of the Baptist was like unfading script*
> *Visible on the unscathed dish.*

This image is static, in spite of its violent fusion of strange elements, but beneath its surface an unknown mode of change seems to be working, so that the effect is both of rest and motion. All these meanings, not so much super-imposed upon as changing into each other, are here gathered together. The poetry in this third version is quite unlike that in the first two. The effect is not of expansion but rather of an intense compression by means of which several layers of time are fused into one. The sentences are short and condensed, and the whole movement of the verse changes.

This may be seen still better in the next verse of the third version, which begins abruptly with the lines I have already quoted:

> *John. Christ. These I would sing*
> *As I have sung Hercules.*

At this point Hölderlin brings in the island of Patmos in a passage where both Hercules and John are allusively indicated, an extremely difficult passage which I shall not try to render. Then he continues, referring to his desire to sing of Christ as he had sung of Hercules:

> *But that*
> *Cannot be. A destiny is different. More marvellous*
> *To sing, richer. Immeasurable*
> *The fable since Him. And now*
> *I would sing the journey of the nobles*
> *To Jerusalem, and anguish wandering in Canossa,*
> *And Henry. Except courage itself*
> *Fail me. That must*
> *Be taken into account. For like morning mist are*
> *   the names*
> *Since Christ. Become dreams. Fall like error.*
> *   On the heart, and deadly if no one*
> *   Ponder what they are and understand.*

It is impossible in a translation to give any idea of the expressiveness of this passage, in which the images of time seem to crowd in so thickly on the poet that he can only mention them in passing, until at last he finds an image for them in something itself without number (I have translated it as 'morning mist': in the original it is 'Morgenluft', 'morning air'). To give an idea of the construction of these lines I must quote them in the original:

> *Wie Morgenluft sind nämlich die Namen*
> *Seit Christus. Werden Träume. Fallen wie Irrtum.*
> *Auf das Herz und tötend, wenn nicht einer*
> *Erwäget, was sie sind und begreift.*

If one did not know who wrote them one would say that they were taken from the later poetry of Rilke. Rilke would have used the image of the morning air in the same way, and

> *Werden Träume. Fallen wie Irrtum*

is exactly in his style. But the pressure of imagination is more solid than Rilke's and the expression more inevitable and less ingenious: ingenuity was Rilke's besetting sin. The psychological development of the passage is extraordinarily moving: beginning with Hölderlin's wish to sing the journey to Jerusalem 'und das Leiden irrend in Canossa' (obviously images of a thousand other things that crowded into his mind), which is followed by the fear that his courage might fail him, and at last by the vision of the names since Christ, which makes the enterprise impossible.

Instead of singing the journey to Jerusalem or counting the names since Christ, he therefore turns to the figure of Christ Himself and to his second version of the poem and his more spacious style. There follows a description of the Last Supper, where Christ speaks of death and perfect love, 'affirming what should be affirmed'.

> *But His light was*
> *Death. For small is the rage of the world.*
> *This He knew. All is good. Thereupon He died.*

Nevertheless, the disciples did not want to leave Him: 'therefore He sent them the Spirit, and the house shook and the thunder of God rolled far rumbling over their boding heads, foretelling that the heroes of death were assembled'. This, I think, signifies another reappearance of the ancient gods; but then Hölderlin prophesies that like the setting sun Christ will return again. He goes on to ask why Christ should have died and what it can mean 'if the glory of the demi-god and of his people' (another reversion to his first conception of Christ as 'the brother of Hercules')

> *Fade, and even the Most High*
> *Turn away His face*
> *Above, so that nothing*
> *Immortal is to be seen in Heaven more*
> *Or on the green earth.*

In answer he uses the simile of the harvest and the thresher: 'the husks fall round his feet, but in the end comes the grain'.

> *For the divine work is as ours.*
> *Not all will the Most High at one time.*

This period of darkness and sterility cannot be alleviated by false hopes or false words, for most hateful to the Lords of Heaven

> *Is falsehood so long as they reign, for then*
> *Manhood is known no more among men.*
> *They do not rule, undying Fate rules,*
> *And its work proceeds of itself*
> *And quickly comes to an end.*

But when the heavenly progress turns higher a redeeming sign is sent, 'and that is the staff of song shining downwards, for nothing is common'.

In this part of the poem, which I have had to summarise very briefly, there is implicit a philosophy of history. The destiny of mankind is pictured as following a cycle resembling that of the terrestrial year with its summer and winter. The world's ages of darkness are prefigured in the life of the disciples after they have lost their Master, when they 'live in loving night, steadfastly preserving in simple eyes abysses of wisdom'. This patient preservation of a light no longer manifest is man's task in ages of darkness, such as Hölderlin considered his own to be. But in the second-last verse he rises above this conception in a fine image:

> But if the heavenly ones
> Love me, as I believe,
> How much more Thee,
> For one thing I know,
> That the will of the Eternal Father
> Pointed to Thee. Quiet is His sign
> In the thundering sky. And One stands beneath
> His life long. For still lives Christ.
> But they have come, the heroes
> His sons, and the holy scriptures
> From Him, and the lightning declares
> The deeds of the world till now,
> A combat unceasing. But He is there. For His works
> Are known to Him from everlasting.

The poem ends with a complaint that the glory of the Heavenly One should have been invisible for so long, and a declaration that the Father 'who rules over all things loves chiefly that the Word should be fostered, signifying inherited good'. 'From this comes German song', he ends. But the core of the poem is in the image of God's quiet sign in the thundering sky and Christ standing beneath it His life long. For that image transforms from beginning to end the conception of history as a cycle of light and darkness.

In a short essay it is possible to deal with only one or two aspects of this poem, which would really require a commentary. It is interesting as one of the first modern poems, in the sense that it envisages human life in historical terms. Where human life is envisaged in historical terms purely the result is confusion and falsehood; and there is evidence that in his prophetic poetry, and in *Patmos* itself, this problem troubled Hölderlin. But while preserving his image of life as a cycle of alternating light and darkness, he saved himself from the blank relativity to which that would have committed him by the vision of the sign of God standing still in the thundering sky.

> *Und Einer steht darunter*
> *Sein Leben lang.*

His belief in Christ was clearly different from the orthodox Christian belief, and it did not force him to deny the ancient gods, who return in the very last verse of the poem. Nevertheless, Christ was the one symbol which united for him the two truths which he perceived in existence: a truth transcending time, and a truth immanent in time: permanence and alternation. The two images in which that union is most strikingly expressed, the one in terms of time, the other in terms of eternity, are those of the head of John the Baptist and of Christ standing beneath the sign of the Father. Such mysteries are beyond the reach of a historical philosophy or of the historical sense. Much of modern poetry has been profoundly influenced by these two things. Much of Hölderlin's was too, but while acknowledging the validity of history he took a step beyond history.

To grasp its nature, to show by what means and in what sense Hölderlin transcended the relativity of history, one must understand his conception of poetry. It is expressed in the poem itself. When the heavenly progress turns higher, he says, a redeeming sign is sent, 'and that is the staff of song shining downwards, for nothing is common'. By song here he obviously does not mean poetry in general, but rather something resembling Blake's Imagination, which he conceives as the instrument of a process that in this world is history and in eternity is the Father's will. It was the function of poetry to seize that unity and make it known as an imaginatively coherent whole. Such glorification of poetry is sometimes regarded as a romantic delusion, along with Wordsworth's and Coleridge's conception of the imagination, with which it has much in common. But it has also much in common with Dante's and Milton's and, above all, Plato's conception of poetry. The kind of poetry which claims to reveal divine mysteries is one of the oldest known to us. In modern times *The Divine Comedy* and *Paradise Lost* explicitly lay claim to a revelation of this kind. That revelation, being in both cases grounded on dogma, was in a sense sanctioned. The mysteries which Hölderlin claimed to reveal were unsanctioned, and in his poetry he treated the gods and human life in much the same way as Plato treated them in the poetic fables which he introduced into *Phaedrus* and *The Banquet*. These fables were imaginative interpretations of mysteries which could not be elucidated by philosophical argument. Hölderlin's prophetic poetry is of the same kind. He approached the mystery of time and eternity through the imagination. He attacked it directly; the mystery itself, not any particular manifestation of it, was his theme; and what he made out of it was a mythology.

ROBERT BROWNING

ABT VOGLER is a good example of Browning's poetic method, and also of a fault into which it sometimes led him: what is usually described as his optimism. In *Abt Vogler*, as in most of his poems, he starts with a fact of experience—in this case the evocation of music from a musical instrument—and follows it to see where it will lead him. He follows it within a simple, impressive framework which is his world of imagination; and no matter in what direction the enquiry may lead him, it is bound to reach and rest upon one of the four truths which to him were the corner-stones of that world. These four truths or affirmations, which depend upon and follow from each other, are—the uniqueness of personality, the imperfection of human life, the desire of the imperfect being for perfection, and the presence of God. These are traditional truths, and all Browning's poetry is in a sense an illustration of them, or rather a description of moments in which one or other of them is realised in ordinary experience.

Browning's enquiry into life ends at some such point; but it may begin anywhere. In general, the farther from the end it begins, the better the result is likely to be. The poems in which he states a point of view quite different from his own, as in *Cleon, Caliban upon Setebos*, and that very fine poem, *An Epistle*, are his best, for they call out and exercise his imagination. Where he has to state a point of view virtually his own, he acquires a false confidence, as in *Rabbi ben Ezra* and to some extent in *Abt Vogler*; the figure who is ostensibly monologising fades into that of the author; and we are confronted with Browning himself and his chief fault, which is to 'greet the Unseen with a cheer' and bluff himself by a display of pious geniality into mystical high spirits. When he says in this mood, '. . . All we have willed or hoped or dreamed of good shall exist', he is not uttering a mystical truth, but expressing his own sanguine and belligerent character. He has given us his impression of that character in the Epilogue to *Asolando*:

> One who never turned his back but marched breast forward,
> Never doubted clouds would break,
> Never dreamed, though right were worsted, wrong would
>   triumph,
> Held we fall to rise, are baffled to fight better,
> Sleep to wake.

This belligerent confidence, a quality of character, was accepted by Browning's contemporaries as optimism. But the great majority of his poems, and the best of them, do not end in belligerent confidence. His character, and his personal philosophy when he stated it, were optimistic; but his world of imagination was not: for the qualities which made up that world were not all comforting. The uniqueness and separation of the individual, the imperfection of human life, are not comforting. One of his finest short poems, *Two in the Campagna*, describes the desire of a lover to be completely united in soul and mind with his mistress, and his frustration:

> *Just when I seemed about to learn!*
>   *Where is the thread now? Off again*
> *The old trick! Only I discern—*
>   *Infinite passion, and the pain*
>   *Of finite hearts that yearn.*

If we judge Browning by his best work, then it is as absurd to call him an optimist as it would be to call Dante an optimist because the *Divine Comedy* begins in Hell and ends in Heaven. What happened to him when he spoke directly of his hopes was that he forgot the more formidable elements in his imaginative world. He had to enter into the lives of people quite unlike himself before he could realise all the obstacles to his easy faith in things. But this is what he did; his work consisted in this.

To understand Browning's originality one has to replace him in his age, an age when the tradition of romantic poetry was generally accepted, and poetry had become overwhelmingly contemplative, and contemplative of a set order of things, such as youth, age, life, death, love, joy, grief. These things were seen as states in an unchanging light; as simple and profound things, not as complex things containing contradictions and subject to change and development. The mood of this poetry is perfectly expressed in Tennyson's lines:

> *The woods decay, the woods decay and fall,*
> *The vapours weep their burthen to the ground,*
> *Man comes and tills the field and lies beneath,*
> *And after many a summer dies the swan.*

The task of the poet was to contemplate such things. Browning instead set himself to enter into them and discover where they would lead him. To call his method dramatic is somewhat to misstate it. The pattern of drama is created by the action. Browning's pattern, as we have seen, was laid up in heaven: the action might receive confirmation from it, but could not create it. This pattern existed for him by an act of faith before he entered into his characters; and each of these was merely a thread by following which he reached some point in the pattern, and in reaching it confirmed concretely the truth of his faith in it. There is this sense of metaphysical activity behind the scenes in all his poetry. The confirmation demanded as many *independent* witnesses as possible. These had to be men and women who had tested themselves against life, and who therefore belonged to all sorts of active callings, as painters, musicians, craftsmen, priests, soldiers, revolutionaries, impostors, lovers, husbands, wives. The particular response, the demonstration of the special kind of truth which fascinated Browning, could not have been elicited from them in the actual moment of action. He did not try to write drama and fail; he tried to do something different, with complete success. He was concerned with the *dramatis personae* rather than the play; he set himself to find out what the *dramatis personae* really thought of the play, privately. The form he invented for discovering this was the dramatic monologue which he perfected in the three volumes written in his fresh maturity: *Dramatic Romances and Lyrics*, *Men and Women*, and *Dramatis Personae*. He used it later, on a vast scale, in *The Ring and the Book*; and the five chief monologues in that long poem contain, perhaps, his greatest poetry.

But if Browning had not been intensely interested in men and women as well as in their place in the pattern, his work would not have its endless fascination and variety. His interest was shown in two ways: in a love for the curious, and in a love for the violently ordinary. He wrote about Paracelsus, Master Hugues of Saxe-Gotha, Abt Vogler and Ben Karshook. He wrote also on such subjects as 'Up at a Villa—Down in the City', 'By the Fireside', 'Any Wife to Any Husband', 'Respectability', 'How it Strikes a Contemporary', 'Popularity', 'Nationality in Drinks', and 'Mr. Sludge, "The Medium"'. His taste for the ordinary shocked his contemporaries more than his taste for the odd and the remote; for it brought unexpected material into his poetry, and along with it, to deal with it, a vast new vocabulary in which the conventional poetic vocabulary of the time was swamped and drowned. The nature of his interest in mankind made this vocabulary necessary; for it was not an interest in human states, such as grief of happiness, but rather in human activity; and all human activity is technical, and demands from the poet a technical interest. Browning had this technical interest in a high degree; when he wrote of painters, or priests, or lovers, or impostors, he wrote with a professional appreciation of their modes. As love was to him the highest activity of which human beings were capable, he devoted his most intense imaginative consideration to it. He wrote, unlike the romantic poets, as a practised lover; and his subject was neither happy nor unhappy love, but love as an experience, a love both ideal and physical, whose reality was bound up with its permanence. Even his most spontaneous lyrics give an impression of experience; but his greatest love poetry is reflective, as in *Two in the Campagna* and *By the Fireside.*

Of a special kind of poetry he was incapable. He was unable to relapse into the passive and receptive states which give a quite different response to life from his own. He could not have seen with composure Tennyson's man come and till the field and lie beneath; he would have concentrated on the tilling of the field, with an agricultural passion. But what his imagination did grasp, that is the various branches of the technique of living, it grasped with a knowledge which no other modern poet has equalled.

All Browning's work is an enquiry beginning with a Perhaps and converging circuitously upon one of the cardinal truths in which he believed. The metrical forms which he uses sometimes fit with astonishing felicity the spirit of this enquiry; they have a tentative and casual music in which the thought seems to be experimentally finding its proper expression: almost a hand-to-mouth music. He was particularly fond of the five-line stanza which he used in *Two in the Campagna* and *By the Fireside*, a stanza in which the last line seems to be carelessly improvised in response to an afterthought. Except when he is using a long heavy line for some dignified theme, the greatest virtue of his verse is naturalness and lightness:

> *How say you? Let us, O my dove,*
> *Let us be unashamed of soul,*
> *As earth lies bare to heaven above!*
> *How is it under our control*
> *To love or not to love?*

This is almost a chance music, cast off in the heat of the enquiry. Of this free, faintly interrogative, street music, he was a master; and he used it with consummate ease and variety. His blank verse had a variety beyond that of any other poet of his age. A few passages from *The Ring and the Book*, where it displays all its qualities, will show what he could do with it:

> *And where was I found but in a strange bed*
> *In a strange room like hell, roaring with noise,*
> *Ruddy with flame, and filled with men. . . .*

> *Launching her looks forth, letting looks reply*
> *As arrows to a challenge. . . .*

> *Found myself in my horrible house once more,*
> *After a colloquy . . . no word assists!*
> *With the mother and the brothers, stiffened me*
> *Strait out from head to foot as dead man does,*
> *And, thus prepared for life as he for hell,*
> *Marched to the public square and met the world. . . .*

> *The two, three creeping house-dog-servant-things*
> *Born mine and bred mine. . . .*

Be as the angels rather, who, apart,
Know themselves into one, are found at length
Married, but marry never. . . .

As in his arms he caught me and, you say,
Carried me in, that tragical red eve,
And laid me where I next returned to life
In the other red of morning, two red plates
That crushed together, crushed the time between,
And are since then a solid fire to me. . . .

The imagery in these passages, and Browning's imagery in general, derives its force from its psychological truth, not from its formal beauty. It shows the depths to which Browning's imagination could pierce; it is sufficient to demonstrate that his view of life cannot be adequately defined as optimism. His variety is another matter; in that, he is second among English poets to no one but Shakespeare and Chaucer.

THE NOVELS OF THOMAS HARDY

HARDY takes a short cut to tragedy by reducing life to a formula. He gets rid beforehand of the main obstacle to tragedy, which is man's natural inclination to avoid it. His characters are passive, or at the best endlessly patient. He does not believe that character is fate; so that for him tragedy does not proceed from action, but resides with the power which determines all action. Misfortune is not brought about by men and women, but is arranged by this power which is indifferent to all arrangements and therefore to misfortune itself. Misfortune is a principle of the universe and falls upon the weak and the strong indiscriminately, neither averted by wisdom nor brought on by folly, striking inevitably and yet as if by chance. For it is the result of a mistake which man cannot correct, since he did not make it. It was made by the Maker of the universe.

In *Wuthering Heights* the action produces the catastrophe. The outcome is inevitable because Cathy and Heathcliff are what they are. We do not have to postulate a malevolent President of the Immortals. But Clym Yeobright and Eustacia Vye and Damon Wildeve in *The Return of the Native* are not the real agents of their tragedy. Behind them, there is a power which insidiously deranges the action and defeats their intentions. Their intentions are generally good. But into the execution a disastrous change enters from outside as by a mathematical law, turning good into ill. This chance is generally a coincidence, and coincidence is therefore an organic part of

Hardy's world, which could not exist without it. Coincidence is indispensable to him, for it is the one device by which he can evoke a sense of this power outside human life which perpetually arranges and deranges it.

The structure of Hardy's novels is designed, therefore, to give an exact value to chance and coincidence. This makes it unusually elaborate, for as the tragedy is not brought about by the action of the characters, they have to be manœuvred into some relation to one another where it will result. If Hardy had written *King Lear*, the old King would have been shorn of his train and shut out in the storm by a complicated series of misunderstandings, and his daughters would have felt bewildered by his strange conduct. A plot which accounted for all these mischances would obviously have to be elaborate. It would also alter the balance of the action, and our response to it. Compared with the implied malignancy in the texture of things, Lear's folly and his daughters' ingratitude would become secondary and unimportant. This environing fate determines the framework of the Wessex novels.

What is this power whose malice Hardy builds into the structure of his novels? Partly it is an imaginative projection of nature as the mid-Victorian geologists and biologists conceived it: something featureless and indifferent which extends through vast processes reaching back past Adam's little world, but also shows itself in the life of the present day as the struggle for existence and the survival of the fittest. Hardy's sensibility was almost as fine as Wordsworth's; but he had read Darwin:

There was now a distinct manifestation of morning in the air, and presently the bleared white visage of a sunless winter day emerged like a dead-born child. . . . Owls that had been catching mice in the outhouses, rabbits that had been eating the winter-greens in the gardens, and stoats that had been sucking the blood of the rabbits, discerning that their human neighbours were on the move, discreetly withdrew from publicity, and were seen and heard no more till nightfall.

That is very unlike nature as Wordsworth saw it, one impulse from which tells us more of human evil and good than all the sages can. It is stripped, empty, indifferent, yet the final director of man's fate.

Hardy's conception of man's relation to the indifferent earth and the indifferent universe is summarised with geometrical precision at the beginning of *The Return of the Native*. The book begins with a description of Egdon Heath, the stage on which the characters will move later on. At the highest point of the heath there is a barrow:

This bossy projection of earth above its natural level occupied the loftiest ground of the loneliest height that the heath contained. Although from the vale it looked but as a wart on an Atlantean brow, its actual bulk was great. It formed the pole and axis of the heathery world.

As the resting man looked at the barrow he became aware that its summit, hitherto the highest object in the whole prospect round, was surmounted by something higher. It rose from the semi-globular mound like a spike from a helmet. . . . It seemed a sort of last man . . . musing for a moment before dropping into eternal night with the rest of his race.

There the form stood, motionless as the hill beneath. Above the plain rose the hill, above the hill rose the barrow, and above the barrow rose the figure. Above the figure was nothing that could be mapped elsewhere than on a celestial globe.

Such a perfect, delicate, and necessary finish did the figure give to the dark pile of hills that it seemed to be the only obvious justification of their outline. Without it, there was the dome without the lantern; with it the architectural demands of the mass were satisfied. The scene was strangely homogeneous, in that the vale, the upland, the barrow and the figure above it amounted only to unity. Looking at this or that member of the group was not observing a complete thing, but a fraction of a thing.

The form was so much like an organic part of the whole motionless structure that to see it move would have impressed the mind as a strange phenomenon. . . .

Yet that is what happened. The figure perceptibly gave up its fixity, shifted a step or two, and turned round. As if alarmed, it descended on the right side of the barrow, with the glide of a water-drop down a bud, and then vanished. The movement had been sufficient to show clearly the characteristics of the figure, and that it was a woman's.

Here we have an exact image of mankind's position in the universe as Hardy saw it. The figure rising from the barrow is the final Euclidean touch to the landscape, and it seems at first an organic part of the entire motionless structure. Then it moves, it reveals itself as human with a volition of its own, and is suddenly 'alarmed'. To the earth and the surrounding universe it has a whole system of relations, some obvious, some inconceivably subtle and remote. But all these relations have one distinguishing character: that the human partner to them feels intense emotion ranging from worship to terror, and the other a sovereign indifference. The indifference is stronger than the worship and the terror. This is the ground of the tragedy, which is that of a little human family caring for love, goodness, pity and honour, but invested by a power which knows nothing of them. For his image of this power Hardy drew partly on the Greek tragic poets who had moved him so deeply as a young man, and partly on the scientific conceptions of his own time, which provided him with a universe stripped of God. Wordsworth had read in the unfettered clouds and the regions of the Heavens the workings of one mind:

> the features
> Of the same face, blossoms upon one tree;
> Characters of the great Apocalypse,
> The types and symbols of Eternity,
> Of first, and last, and midst, and without end.

In place of these Hardy saw a featureless, blossomless, characterless, illegible presence. This is the power that man fights single-handed. He does not fight other men but the common enemy of man, who is everywhere.

In this combat Hardy is on the side of man, for man is better than the universe that defeats him. Yet to say that he is on the side of man does not put the case strongly enough; he is partial to man in a special way. By his capacity to feel and judge his feelings, to see the past and plan for the future, man should be the centre of creation, yet he is not; and the fact that he is not is an obscure anomaly, an injustice, the original injustice. If God were immanent in the universe the injustice could be rectified; divine breathings, grace, aid, comfort could come to man from every side; impulses from a vernal wood which would tell him more human evil and good than all the sages can. But God is absent; the universe is indifferent; no help can come from it, but only accident and disaster; and the prevision which should have made man its collaborator merely makes him its more complete victim, since prevision is useless. Sometimes we have the feeling in reading Hardy that the universe is taking a private revenge on man because, alone among its creatures, he can see it as it is, reason about it, and demonstrate its cruelty. There would be no one to embarrass it in its course of evil if it were not for this unwanted bastard child who sees too much. In Hardy's universe man's presence is ultimately inexplicable; so that while he sees nature as indifferent, he cannot help personifying it in some diabolical form. This is a measure of the intensity of his feelings towards it, and of the contradiction of his thought. To him man's position can be explained only by a universe which perpetually defeats him, unintentionally yet intentionally. The universe, seen in this way, is simply another term for evil.

Hardy lifted evil from man's shoulders and laid it on the universe. 'And he told me', says Gammer Oliver in *The Woodlanders*, 'that no man's hands could help what they did, any more than the hands of a clock.'

This evil, which is only accident, is everywhere in nature as in human life:

> On older trees still . . . huge lobes of fungi grew like lungs. Here, as everywhere, the Unfulfilled Intention, which makes life what it is, was as obvious as it could be among the depraved crowds of a slum. The leaf was deformed, the curve was crippled, the taper was interrupted; the lichen ate the vigour of the stalk, and the ivy slowly strangled to death the promising sapling.

Accident or chance, then, is at the heart of Hardy's world, for man is the most unaccountable accident of all: midway between the creation and the point where God once was—suspended between nature and nothingness. What supports him there, and how he got there, are questions which Hardy can answer only by personifying nothingness itself (that nothingness which once had been God), and attributing to it will and enmity. He has to hate it because he loves man. But it is hard to tell whether his love is a reflection of his hate, or his hate of his love. They are inextricably bound together; he cannot express the one without implying the other; his love is never pure acceptance. Consequently it can sometimes become perverse and corrupt, as in the passage where the President of the Immortals has his last joke with poor Tess.

Hardy's greatness, in the novels particularly, is a mixed greatness. The passage in *The Return of the Native* describing Mrs. Yeobright's walk back across the heath after being turned away from her son's door illustrates this mixed character of his imagination. On her way she meets a little boy who trots beside her, staring curiously into her face.

''Tis a long way home, my child, and we shall not get there till evening.'

'I shall,' said her small companion. 'I am going to play marnels afore supper, and we go to supper at six o'clock, because father comes home. Does your father come home at six too?'

'No; he never comes; nor my son either, nor anybody.'

'What have made you so down? Have you seen a ooser?'

'I have seen what's worse—a woman's face looking at me through a window-pane.' . . .

'You must be a very curious woman to talk like that.'

'O no, not at all,' she said, returning to the boy's prattle. 'Most people who grow up and have children talk as I do. When you grow up your mother will talk as I do too.'

'I hope she won't; because 'tis very bad to talk nonsense.'

'Yes, child; it is nonsense, I suppose. Are you not nearly spent with the heat?'

'Yes. But not so much as you be.'

'How do you know?'

'Your face is white and wet, and your head is hanging-down-like.'

The boy leaves Mrs. Yeobright sitting in the middle of the heath and asks her what he should tell his mother. Mrs. Yeobright answers:

'Tell her you have seen a broken-hearted woman cast off by her son.'

This is the height to which Hardy can rise when coincidence has engineered his characters into a tragic situation. But how did Mrs. Yeobright get there? By a fantastic series of misunderstandings in which there was no substance; for her son Clym had not turned her away, and his wife Eustacia did not really wish her ill. The little house where this false tragedy was concocted, with Clym fast asleep in one room, Eustacia and her former lover Wildeve whispering in the other, and Mrs. Yeobright knocking at the door, resembles a setting of one of those farces where figures keep unexpectedly popping out of bedroom wardrobes. Yet a whole sequence of disasters follows from this

scene, including the death of Mrs. Yeobright, Eustacia
and Wildeve.

Hardy's tragic scenes have this mixture of poetry and
absurdity. But the evocations of the remote relations
between man and indifferent nature by which he prepares
for them show a wonderful delicacy and truth. A fine
example is the passage in *The Woodlanders* where Giles
Winterborne and Marty South plant the young pines.

> 'How they sigh directly we put 'em upright, though while
> they are lying down they don't sigh at all,' said Marty.
> 'Do they?' said Giles. 'I've never noticed it.'
> She erected one of the young pines into its hole, and held up
> her finger; the soft musical breathing instantly set in, which was
> not to cease night or day till the grown tree should be felled—
> probably long after the two planters had been felled themselves.

Even in describing passionate love Hardy strikes this
remote, faintly menacing note, through which sounds the
indifference of the universe.

> Clym and Eustacia, in their little house at Alderworth, beyond
> East Egdon, were living on with a monotony which was delight-
> ful to them. The heath and changes of weather were quite
> blotted out from their eyes for the present. They were enclosed
> in a sort of luminous mist, which hid from them surroundings of
> any inharmonious colour, and gave to all things the character of
> light. When it rained, they were charmed, because they could
> remain indoors together all day with such a show of reason; when
> it was fine they were charmed, because they could sit together on
> the hills. They were like those double stars which revolve round
> each other, and from a distance seem to be one. The absolute
> solitude in which they lived intensified their reciprocal thoughts;
> yet some might have said that it had the disadvantage of con-
> suming their mutual affections at a fearfully prodigal rate.

He conveys into a description of light falling on a woman's
face a sense of the distant relation between her and the sun
which mechanically shines on her and mechanically takes
away its light again.

When she looked down sideways . . . she became pretty, and even handsome, particularly that in the action her features caught slantwise the rays of the strongly coloured sun, which made transparencies of her eyelids and nostrils, and set fire on her lips.

Hardy's massive tragic effects are built up on numerous minute perceptions such as these.

Hardy was partial to man; to be partial is to be involuntarily unjust; and in taking evil from man's shoulders he robbed him of one of his indispensable possessions. For in relieving man of evil he did not improve his situation, but made it worse, since he concentrated all evil against him. His characters, therefore, are curiously neutral; they gain colour only when passion of misfortune touches them, and are quite convincing only in their helplessness and instability. He draws women better than men. He sees woman and her response to love almost with a woman's eyes. He is on woman's side against man, just as he is on man's side against nature, and for the same reason; for woman is the final victim. He drew one man of strong and active character, Michael Henchard in *The Mayor of Casterbridge*. But most of his men are simple or priggish or effeminate. Their highest virtue is uncomplaining endurance of misfortune, a virtue which they share with women. In describing endurance Hardy is best, for by enduring man seems to rise above the malice of fate by a pure act of magnanimity comprehensible only to himself. The peasants who form a chorus to the novels are the final expression of this endurance, which has become so native to them that it has been transformed into a kind of humour. They are too low to fear a fall. They are in the position where the universe wants to have them; therefore beyond the reach of tragedy: the speakers of the epilogue to every action.

FRANZ KAFKA

KAFKA starts with a general or universal situation, not a particular one. This being so, it does not matter where he begins his story, for the situation is always there, and always the same. He does not have to wait, like most writers, for some incident, some human entanglement, to strike his imagination. A mere subject for a story in the ordinary sense, indeed, would cramp his powers; he would feel it as a constraint. In his diary he notes that when he tries to write on a set theme he is quite at a loss, but that as soon as he scribbles down a sentence such as 'He stood at the window and looked down at the street', he knows he is right. It is one of the quite ordinary doors through which he can enter the universal situation. Emerson says, 'The way to the centre is everywhere equally short', and Kafka might have echoed the thought in a different intonation.

As the situation is universal and stationary, it is also storyless; and this is the point at which Kafka's art begins. He is a great story-teller because there is no story for him to tell; so that he has to make it up. No foundation in fact, no narrative framework, no plot or scene for a plot is there to help him; he has to create the story, character, setting and action, and embody in it his meaning. But there a difficulty arises. For the meaning of a universal situation is inexhaustible; the story can, and actually should, go on for ever; whether it ends or not is unimportant. In his three great stories the endings are indicated, but there are gaps in the story, how great or how small it is impossible to say; and this does not matter.

His stories generally begin in the midway of life, at a point decided by the chance of the moment, and yet at a decisive point, since in the universal situation every point is decisive. The image of a road comes into our minds when we think of his stories; for in spite of all the confusions and contradictions in which he was involved he held that life was a way, not a chaos, that the right way exists and can be found by a supreme and exhausting effort, and that whatever happens every human being in fact follows some way, right or wrong. The road then is there; we may imagine beside it a wayside inn from which an anonymous figure is just emerging. He looks ahead and sees, perhaps on a distant hill, a shape which he has often seen before in his journey, but always far away, and apparently inaccessible; that shape is justice, grace, truth, final reconciliation, father, God. As he gazes at it he wonders whether he is moving towards it while it is receding from him, or flying from it while it is pursuing him. He is tormented by this question, for it is insoluble by human reasoning. He feels irresistibly drawn towards that distant shape, and yet cannot overcome his dread of it. Kafka describes in *The Castle* the struggle to reach it, and in *The Trial* the flight from it. But the hero can neither reach it nor escape it, for it is enveloped in a mystery different from the ordinary mystery of human life, and he does not know the law of that mystery. The roads leading towards it are therefore deceitful; the right turn may easily chance to be the wrong, and the wrong the right. In his greatest story Kafka tells how the hero sets out on a road which seems to be leading straight to the Castle, the dwelling-place of divinity, but how after walking for a long time he finds that though it appears to be making towards the Castle it never brings him any nearer. This or something like this happens innumerable times in his stories; it may almost be said, indeed, that nothing but this happens; though the situation conceals itself behind so many veils that the event, when it occurs, always seems novel and unique.

The frustration of the hero is an intrinsic part of Kafka's theme; and it is caused by what in theological language is known as the irreconcilability of the divine and the human law; a subtle yet immeasurable disparity. Out of this dilemma Kafka fashions his stories, or rather his story, for it is one story; he has nothing else to tell. He was confirmed in his reading of it by his study of Kierkegaard, but he must himself have made that reading independently, for his whole unhappy upbringing was behind it, and particularly his relation to his father whom he could never reach, and from whom, until he was nearly forty, he could never escape. When as a young man, with a young man's metaphysical passion, he universalised this situation, he fashioned God in his father's image. At thirty-seven he at last made a great settlement with his father in an inordinately long, eloquent letter where, having stated his case, he went on with equal scrupulousness to state his father's. Afterwards the compulsive tie binding him to his father seems to have eased, and his conception of the universal situation became less massively pessimistic. The change can be seen in the stories which he wrote during the last few years of his life, where there is an approach to serenity. In his letter to his father he used the same method as he had employed in *The Castle* and *The Trial*; for what is so striking in them is the care he takes to state both sides of the problem: man's side, and God's.

But the supreme originality of Kafka's work does not lie in his reading of the universal position, which he shared with Kierkegaard at some points, but in his story-telling, by means of which he created a world. He is a great story-teller both by his art and by the interest and value of what he says. And the value of what he says does not depend on the truth of his metaphysical structure, any more than the value of what Dante says depends on his theology. We can read *The Castle* and *The Trial* rejecting his theory of the irreconcilability of divine and human law, and yet find in them the most enchanting discoveries, the most startling riddles, the most profound insights into human life. It is these that give his work its endless interest: the meta-physical structure, impressive as it is, is only a structure. But he enchants us equally by his art. To read him is to realise what the craft of story-telling exists for. Though modern realistic practice may conceal the fact, it is clear that story-telling is essentially a matter of invention; for all that any writer can start with is a mere narrative frame-work, and invention of scene and detail and dialogue alone can give it life. Kafka does not have even a narrative framework; so that the story becomes invention and noth-ing else. And though this may seem a drawback, it is really an advantage; for the invention, being new by necessity, is endlessly surprising, as invention should be. The scenes and figures and conversations seem to rise out of nothing, since nothing resembling them was there before. We con-template them as we contemplate things which we see for the first time. As they exist in a world which is strange to us, the narrator has to describe them with minute exacti-tude; and from this necessity springs one of the most delightful graces of Kafka's art, his circumstantiality. To describe circumstantially a railway station or a large hotel or a public-house would weary us, since we are likely to know them; but Kafka's detail is more like that of a travel book which recounts minutely the customs, dresses and utensils of some newly discovered tribe; everything is strange. Besides, each detail in these stories has a purpose, and tells us something which has to be told, and is an intrinsic part of the story. Or of the structure; for *The Castle* and *The Trial* are not only stories, but edifices built according to a metaphysical specification. As the story proceeds the edifice rises.

The hero of the two great stories is anybody, and his story is the story of anybody. 'Anybody' is obviously an allegorical figure, fit to be designated as K. or Josef K., as Kafka names the heroes of *The Castle* and *The Trial*. Yet these stories are not allegories. The truths they bring out are surprising or startling, not conventional and expected, as the truths of allegory tend to be. They are more like serious fantasies; the spontaneous expression of Kafka's genius was fantasy, as his early short stories show. Fantasy came as naturally to him as writing. In *The Castle* and *The Trial* he employs it for purposes as serious as any writer has ever attempted. But no designation of his art is satisfying. We can see what it was not; to find a name for it is of little consequence.

OSWALD SPENGLER

OSWALD SPENGLER once had a great vogue in Germany. He first became known in England when volume one of his chief work, *The Downfall of the West* (Der Untergang des Abendlandes), was translated after the 1914–18 war. It was not so well received as in Germany: some of the reviews were adverse; but the majority were respectful or enthusiastic. Spengler's reputation in England was ruined by the translation of his last book, *Years of Decision* (Jahre der Entscheidung), in which he prophesied two centuries of world wars. It was a short book written in a popular style, and in spite of the horrifying prospect which it opened into the future, it stated explicitly the chief heads of Spengler's philosophy of history. I wish in this essay to enquire into one or two aspects of that philosophy.

I had better deal first with Spengler's verbal brutality, which, though it fits his philosophy well enough, is not necessary to it. He is fond of such generalisations as:

> Man is a *beast of prey*. I shall never tire of proclaiming that. All the moralizers and social uplifters who would pretend to be something better are only beasts of prey with their teeth drawn. When I call a man a best of prey whom do I insult, man—or the beast? For the great beasts of prey are consummately noble creatures, and without the hypocrisy of a human morality based on weakness.

The essential thing here is Spengler's inflection, not what he says. Many people before him have held that man is a beast of prey; Hobbes did so. But he did not think it was a noble or edifying fact; he did not romantically exalt the lion, the tiger, and the shark, and exhort man to become like them. This is what Spengler does; beast of prey in his vocabulary is a term of praise; and this fact is only to be accounted for in part by his philosophy of history, and requires further explanation. The explanation, I think, is that he belongs to a special class of writer: the pseudo-man of action. Carlyle, who belonged to it too, occasionally made assertions of a similar kind, and Nietzsche did so fairly often. Real men of action do not write in this way; they can be brutal, but not romantically brutal; they know too much about the human tiger and shark. The pseudo-man of action alone romanticises brutality in this way, and by the pseudo-man of action I do not mean the man who, but for some physical or other incidental defect, might have become a great figure in history, but the man who lives in a dream of action, imagining that by the ardour of his dream he influences events. Carlyle behaves in this way when he exhorts Cromwell at the critical point of battles, forgetting that his exhortations come two centuries too late; Nietzsche, when he constitutes himself the official midwife of a Superman who is never born; and Spengler, when he implies that in writing about history he is in some way making it. A man who is not framed for action will commit the most shocking errors in writing about it and violate the moral sense of ordinary people without being in the least conscious that he is doing so. Carlyle and Nietzsche were in practical capacity below, not above, the average; but they felt a need to identify themselves in some way with action. The result was a sort of sycophancy towards all men who could do things: the attitude of a weak boy to a strong one, or of a country doctor superintending the birth of the young master at the big house. The task of the reason is to judge action; but men like

Carlyle and Nietzsche who live in a vicarious dream of action can only glorify it, betraying reason to their infatuations. Spengler does this too; but his god is not any man of action in particular, but history, which is action generalised; and as he writes of it as a pseudo-man of action, his history is really a dream of history.

A dream of history can be constructed only by a man who knows a good deal of history; and as knowledge is always respectable, such dreams are accorded a greater intellectual estimation than the dream of fair women which inspired one of Tennyson's poems. They postulate, for one thing, 'the historical sense', a modern faculty which is very useful and enjoys a great deal of prestige. The historical sense, as writers like Spengler employ it, envisages human life as a finite phenomenon completely hemmed in by Time. Time determines the forms of human life at different periods, making it a different thing, for instance, in ancient Greece from what it is to-day. Though this is a platitude it is one which in our age has acquired a new importance. But historical time is also a process with laws of its own, by virtue of which civilisations rise, grow, flourish and decay (Spengler's favourite theme) in accordance with a necessity which no human effort can influence; and human life, at any point at which we may consider it, is merely an effect of that process. Everyone who possesses the historical sense does not go to such extremes as this; but Spengler does; he makes of history, or rather of the historical process, the sole significant embodiment of human life, and consistently implies that the individual human existence is not of the slightest consequence.

The best way to show this is to allow him to speak for himself:

'We live in a mighty age. It is the greatest that the culture of the West has ever seen or ever will see, the same that the ancient world knew between Cannae and Actium, the age that produced the splendid names of Hannibal, Scipio, Gracchus, Marius, Sulla, Caesar. The Great War was only the first lightning flash falling from the thunder-cloud which floats, heavy with fate, over this century. *The form of the world* is today being radically remoulded as it was by the nascent Imperium Romanum, without regarding the desires and wishes of "the many", or counting the sacrifices which *every* such decision demands. But who can understand this? Who can endure this thought? Who can feel it a joy to be alive when this is happening? The age is a great one, but its men are correspondingly small. They can no longer endure tragedy, either on the stage or in real life. . . . But the destiny which flung them into this decade has them by the throat and will do with them what must be done, whether they will or no. The cowardly safety of the end of last century is over. *Life as danger*, the *real* life of history, once more enters into its right. . . . Now only the man who *dares*, who has the courage to see and deal with things as they are, really counts. A time is coming—more, it is already here!—which will have no room for sensitive souls and frail ideals. The ancient barbarism which for centuries lay fettered and buried beneath the strict forms of a high culture is awakening again, now that that culture is consummated and civilization has begun: the warlike and healthy joy in a man's own strength, which an age of rationalist thought saturated in literature despised; the unbroken instinct of race, which is resolved to live otherwise than under the oppression of piles of dead books and bookish ideals.'

This is simultaneously a glorification of the Nazi creed, and an intimation that Germany need not put up with its first defeat.

Again it is the bombastic inflection that arrests the attention most loudly; Spengler is so in love with tragedy that anyone who does not welcome it with open arms, whether as torture, mutilation, sudden death, or mere starvation, is not worth his consideration. But the important thing about this passage is that it embodies his view of history, and consequently his view of human life. I shall quote one or two further passages to make this clearer:

In ages of high culture human history is the history of political powers. The form of that history is war. Peace is only another variety of it. It is the continuation of war with other means. . . . Domestic politics exists solely to secure the power and unity of external politics. Where it follows other aims of its own the state begins to decline. . . .

A strong race must not only have an inexhaustible birthrate, but also a rigid process of selection through the hardships of life, accident, sickness and war. The medical science of the nineteenth century, a true product of rationalism, is from this point of view a sign of decadence.

This view of history and of human life is put forward quite seriously and has been accepted by many people. The two most obvious things about it are that it makes no allowance for the moral impulses of mankind, and that it grants no value to individual existence. For it, Christ is non-existent either as a historical figure or as a spiritual reality. Man as an individual exists only in so far as he furthers some change in the perpetual process of change that is called history. And history itself is merely a play of forces, in which one factor, and one factor alone, is decisive: power. This is our life in its essence: the rest is talk, morality, day-dreaming, ideology.

The best way to estimate this view of life is to compare it with one which used to be universal and is still held, I think, by the great majority of people. It accepted as the unit of its general view of human life something temporally far smaller than the units of the historical sense; it saw life as a progress from the cradle to the grave, not as the growth, fruition, decline and downfall of civilisations. It started from the individual but reached the universal, since individuality is the universal form in which human life manifests itself. Accepting individuality as the norm, it sought to discover the nature of the laws which govern the individual existence, and its ultimate meaning. This was a task which carried it beyond history into religion; for the view of life of which I am speaking could not admit that human life was a historical phenomenon and nothing more. Mankind's secular destiny was certainly worked out in history, and history was therefore a process of the utmost significance. But man was also an immortal soul, whose essence could never be seized and contained by history. He had longings which history could not satisfy, and sorrows of which history took no account. He was an actor simultaneously in the historical drama and in another whose terms were strange to history: a drama of sin and atonement, aspiration and failure, which implied a responsibility to something beyond time. On this foundation the old traditional view of human life was based: on man's existence from birth to death, and on immortality. It took into account not only what man succeeded in being on this earth (that is history), but all that he failed to be. History is the record of human limitation; it accepts action effectively operative in time, and nothing more. Religion accepts the totality of human desire, disappointment and fulfilment, whether effectively operative in time or not. Its basis is therefore wider than that of history, though temporally it seems more restricted: the life of a human being from birth to death. Accordingly it could not dismiss morality and individuality as mere trimmings of existence, and assume, as Spengler does, that they are of no importance. It accepted them as essential attributes of human nature, and tried to account for them and give them a meaning.

Now it seems to me that we are seeing to-day a fight between these two views of life: the religious view, which is also that of the artist, and the historical view. The virtue of the first—not its supreme virtue, which is its truth, but its relative pragmatic virtue—is that it gives meaning to the actual life we live, and accounts to us for ourselves. In one of his essays Alexander Blok, the Russian poet, claimed that the time of 'Goodness, Beauty and Truth' was past. That is a typical if extreme utterance of the historical sense, and at the same time an error which could have been avoided by remembering that human life is a life between birth and death, and that in that life the individual, whether civilised or savage, cannot but have some relation, positive or negative, to Goodness, Beauty and Truth. Spengler, politically a bitter enemy of everything Blok believed in, thought here in the same way. To him the one operative factor in existence is not goodness, beauty or truth, but power, and so he praises the beast of prey and pours scorn on 'a human morality based on weakness'. The old view of life sees endless variety and complexity in human existence, and yet makes certain fundamental distinctions: good and evil, truth and falsehood, guilt and innocence. The new historical view as expressed by Spengler sees no essential variety in human existence at all, but only the category of power, or, in other words, of necessity; and yet, in spite of its simplicity, it leads to no conclusion: it remains on the plane of pure relativity. And on the plane of pure relativity it is possible to prefer anything to anything else: a well-grown tiger to Socrates or Christ, brutality to kindness, cunning to honesty, treachery to good faith. One can therefore say with a good conscience: 'The medical science of the nineteenth century, a true product of rationalism, is . . . a sign of decadence', or: 'Few can stand a long war. But nobody could stand a long peace', because one has no palpable human reality to hold on to, and has forgotten the pitiful limitations and the necessary virtues of existence as the individual knows it. So in men without imagination, like Spengler, the spectacle of history can easily rouse an irrational arrogance. The historian who accepts the limitations of ordinary existence may find some matter for grief in contemplating battlefields and massacres; but the feelings of a man who regards history as the sole meaning of human life must be somewhat different, and it may easily be beneath him to 'regard the desires and wishes' or 'count the sacrifices' of 'the many'. And here we come to the point where Spengler's verbal brutality and his philosophy of history meet. A purely relative view of human destiny based on a theory of a play of forces gives an opportunity, indeed a justification, for brutality.

Another danger of a view of life which is not based on the fundamental fact of the individual human existence is that it is extremely susceptible to fashion. The history of Spengler's literary development is instructive. In 1918 Germany was defeated, and a few years later there appeared the first volume of *The Downfall of the West*, proclaiming that all Europe was doomed. After the peace came the German inflation, one of whose effects was that the German peasantry hoarded their produce or profiteered in it, so that a lively antipathy arose between the country and the towns. Presently appeared the second volume of *The Downfall of the West* which prophesied, among other things, that one of the decisive struggles of the future would be the struggle between the country and the towns. But meanwhile Germany had become a tepidly Social Democratic Republic, and Spengler published another book called *Prussianism and Socialism*, in which he tried to show that both political forms were inspired by the same ideal. Then German Social Democracy entered into its swift decline, and with the advent of Hitler Spengler's last book, *Years of Decision*, appeared, which foretold the rise of a whole line of Caesars.

By all this I do not intend to cast any aspersion on

Spengler's honesty, but merely to show that he was a man extremely susceptible to fashion. He was obviously sincere when he complained, in a footnote to his last book, that 'What I described in *Prussianism and Socialism*—and it has almost always been misunderstood—was Socialism *as an ethical attitude*, not as a materialistic economic principle'. Fashion is a sweeping generalisation from insufficient or trivial evidence; and that might be a description of all Spengler's books. The temporary downfall of Germany after the war, enlarged and touched up in his dream of history, became the final downfall of Europe. The appearance of Hitler was sufficient to presume the advent of a whole line of Caesars. A few years were sufficient to change Spengler's conclusions about the whole future of history. Yet these conclusions were formulated as universal truths; facts as incontestable as the latest mode. And this is understandable, for the historical sense must always be revising its conception of history in accordance with the contemporary growth of history. It has no hold on any other reality. And without a hold on some other reality, it is impossible to have a true conception of human existence.

Spengler was an excellent pamphleteer with an astonishing gift for facile generalisation; he was not, as a thinker, of any importance. But he was of some importance as a wholesale dealer in the historical sense, as a man who employed the historical sense with unexampled irresponsibility, so that in his works it can see a caricature of itself. The historical sense is a useful method for viewing human life in the large; but when it edges out every other method, invading not only history, where it is only partially valid, but fiction and poetry as well, it becomes a great danger.

THE POLITICAL VIEW OF
LITERATURE

IN his book, *The Novel and the Modern World*, Mr.
David Daiches gives an excellent statement of what is
called the political view of literature. From that stand-
point he criticises a number of modern novelists, Gals-
worthy, Conrad, Katherine Mansfield, James Joyce, Virginia Woolf and Aldous Huxley. The criticism is sensitive
and closely reasoned. The four essays on Joyce are especially penetrating, for in them Mr. Daiches puts into
practice his counsel to work from the wider context inward
and from the work outward—the wider context being
society. But the working inward determines to a great
extent what he finds in the work itself; it blinds him, for
instance, to the strong Catholic element in Joyce's work.
To him Joyce has always striven to achieve the perfect
work of art—'the work which says all things at once so
that the life he describes is all life, and the words in which
he expresses himself convey no point of view because they
convey all points of view.' There is some truth in this, but
none which can explain why Joyce should write at all; for
no one can write without having some point of view, without seeing life in some terms. The terms in which Joyce
sees life are difficult to define because of his simultaneous
revolt against and attachment to the Catholic Church; his
attempt to describe all life is really an attempt to portray
all Joyce, and his work is a minute, Catholic self-inquisi-
tion conducted in an anti-Catholic or burlesque-Catholic
spirit. But the Catholic impulse in Joyce does not count

for Mr. Daiches, because the wider context from which he works inward does not include Catholicism except as something to be interpreted in political terms.

Within such limits his criticism is thorough. His point of view, on the other hand, and the kind of statement by which he supports it, become more doubtful the more clearly they are formulated. As that point of view is widely held, it may be worth while to consider it. Mr. Daiches 'works inward' from such assumptions as this:

> Unfortunate as we are in many respects in living in the present world rather than in some time in the past, we are at least fortunate in this: that we are living at a time when the state of civilisation is patent to all. No intelligent observer who has not allowed wishful thinking to master his intellectual processes can deny that we are living in the midst of the disintegration of a civilisation, or, to put it in a less terrifying manner (though it is terrifying), in a transitional stage between two civilisations. Rarely, if ever, has the nature of the contemporary situation been so clear to observers. . . . We can look back on the recent past, knowing what it has been leading to, and analyse it with the familiarity of a contemporary, yet with the knowledge which hitherto has been reserved for the future historian. While as a rule the contemporary cannot see the wood for the trees and the historian cannot see the trees for the wood, here is a situation which seems to offer a chance of seeing clearly both the individual trees and the wood as a whole.

A great number of intelligent people would agree without qualification with most of the things which Mr. Daiches says here, and would regard them as truisms. For myself, I cannot feel sure of any of them, except the fairly clear evidence that a disintegration is going on. Whether that is a disintegration of civilisation or of something within civilisation I do not know. Whether in the first case it will lead to another civilisation or to something which cannot properly be called civilisation at all (Fascism, for example), and whether in the second case civilisation will manage to cure the disease within it, no one can possibly know. Mr. Daiches does not say what he means by civilisation; he may mean much the same as politicians mean when they say that this or that will spell the end of civilisation; but I do not think so. As for the nature of the contemporary situation being unusually clear to observers, we may certainly think it is clear, or feel convinced that it is clear; but there is evidence that it is not clear, since it is seen in one set of terms by some intelligent men and in another set by others. Mr. Daiches says that we can see both the wood and the trees, but the trees which Mr. T. S. Eliot sees are not Mr. Daiches' trees. Mr. Daiches is at liberty to say that Mr. Eliot is wrong, but not that his opinions do not exist. Again, whether the future will be fought for between the Fascists and the Communists is becoming more and more doubtful; and in the months since Mr. Daiches wrote his book it has become equally possible to regard the conflict as a conflict between Democracy (what there is of it) and Totalitarianism (all there is of it), or even as a conflict between Christian civilisation and a civilisation founded on a purely secular creed. The contemporary situation, then, is by no means clear; yet the wider context from which Mr. Daiches works inward assumes that it is perfectly clear. This assumption is founded ultimately on some such hypothesis as dialectical materialism which simplifies everything on a vast scale. If a Calvinist critic in the Jacobean age had tried to assess Shakespeare, Donne and Webster in terms of the new dynamic theology, insisting that they could reflect their age only by associating themselves with the rising middle class, the new liberating force in society whose triumph was inevitable, we should have had a situation similar to that which Mr. Daiches imagines the present one to be. In reality, the contemporary situation will not become clear until after the event; we do not know what shape it will have to the future historian; therefore we cannot judge contemporary literature by means of it. Ordinary legitimate scepticism should be enough to tell us this.

To see the contemporary situation as clearly as Mr. Daiches sees it we must simplify a great number of things. This leads Mr. Daiches to ignore Joyce's Catholicism; it also leads him to 'interpret' Eliot's and Huxley's religious beliefs. As this interpretation is typical of a great deal of modern criticism I shall quote it.

> It is interesting to compare T. S. Eliot's wasteland with the wasteland that Huxley paints in his early novels. They have much in common, though Eliot's is the wasteland of the thwarted classicist and Huxley's that of the thwarted romantic. Eliot emphasises lack of pattern and purpose while Huxley stresses lack of worth-whileness for the individuals involved. And ultimately (again, if he does not go crazy first) your thwarted classicist will find refuge in some fairly rigid and institutionalised scheme of things to compensate him for his wounded sense of order. He joins the Roman Catholic Church or, like Eliot, the Anglican Church, which is almost the same thing. Huxley becomes a mystical pacifist with inclinations towards a personal interpretation of Buddhism, whereas Eliot lands up by becoming an orthodox member of a highly ritualistic and hierarchic religion. They represent two complementary types. Both, it may be added, avoid the issue, which is not personal compensation but the alteration of the environment which has produced the necessity for that compensation—the evolution and stabilisation of a standard in which society can believe and with reference to which its activities can be given purpose and meaning and value.

The difficulty of dealing with criticism of this kind is that it entirely ignores the nature of the things it is treating. It assumes that Mr. Eliot's religion is not real religion, and ultimately, perhaps, that religion is itself unreal—the opium of the masses which has now become the opium of the literary classes. It implies that if Mr. Eliot set out to alter his environment, and identified himself with the proletariat, he would have no problems at all. To believe such things is ultimately to believe that we have no personal relations and no personal difficulties in living, but merely the public duty to change our environment, a duty which will bring us allies and enemies and nothing else. Mr. Daiches thinks that Mr. Eliot's religion is merely an avoidance of the issue and a compensation for his real duty; yet how he can believe that after reading *The Waste Land*, *Ash Wednesday* and *The Family Reunion* is past imagining, unless he has read them without believing that they deal with anything that is real. Whoever enters imaginatively into the experience which Mr. Eliot describes in *The Family Reunion* will be greatly surprised to hear his religion called a compensation. Anyone who cannot enter into it is not in a position to understand it; all that he can do, therefore, is to interpret it in his own terms, which are foreign to the terms of the experience itself. Words like 'compensation' are two-edged; Mr. Daiches' interpretation of Mr. Eliot's experience may be a compensation for not understanding it. The first condition of any genuine criticism of Mr. Eliot's religion is that it should be understood; the critic may then decide that it contains truth or contains nothing but error; but he is not entitled to transform it into something else and then assess it as something else. I do not know whether Mr. Daiches would deny that there have been men who have been genuinely religious in the past and that there may be men who are genuinely religious now; the interpretative method of criticism, which deprives everything of its individuality, changing it into something without individuality, can become so strange that one does not know what to expect. But at any rate he seems to be sure that in our own time, when 'rarely if ever has the nature of the contemporary situation been so clear to

observers', Mr. Eliot's religion can be only a compensation.

In this note I am concerned with questioning such
assumptions, for they are hardly ever questioned. No
doubt there is some truth in them, but evidently much
error as well. Most of the error rises from the fact that
such theories are too general to be applied to individual
works of imagination without robbing them of their
individuality. Here is an admirable statement of Mr.
Daiches' theory:

> A work may be many different things at the same time, but
> it is important to know which is the essential thing, what it is
> that determines the pattern and the scale of emphasis, what is the
> real work, and what are the by-products of it. The purely formal
> critic always tends to think that he knows what the work in
> question is simply because it is in print before him. But he is much
> mistaken. The printed text may stand for any number of different
> works, as the history of criticism abundantly shows. What the
> real work is and what gives the principle of organization to the
> whole can be certainly determined only by investigating the
> relation of the printed words to the civilization that produced
> them.

One might agree with this completely if one could be
sure what Mr. Daiches means by the 'real work', and if
one were confident that the relation of the work to the
civilisation which produced it could be ascertained with
any precision. The work itself, as it lies in print before us,
is an exact thing; the civilisation from which it sprang we
can never see with the same immediacy. What happens
when we read a novel? We recognise first, if it is a good
one, that the author is describing real people and real
experience. How do we recognise it? By drawing on our
conscious or guessed-at knowledge of life, not on our
knowledge of historical civilisation. The first impact of
reality comes here, and it comes immediately. The novel

may describe life in the eighteenth century or life to-day; the fact that the novelist is writing of a different period need not prevent us from seeing that he is dealing with real people. This is a fact at which no one would think of wondering, and it requires no explanation. But the work which moves us in this way, Mr. Daiches asserts, is not the real work; to discover that we must establish the relation of the book we are reading to the civilisation from which it sprang. It is true that we shall not understand the book properly unless we do that, and unless we establish its position in the general course of literature. This can never be done completely, but the more we know about the historical genesis and position of a book the better we shall understand it. This is obvious. Where I disagree with Mr. Daiches is where he says that the 'real' work is discovered by investigating the book's genesis in the civilisation which produced it; for he seems to imply that our first actual experience of it—whatever it may be— *Tristram Shandy* or *Wuthering Heights* or *The Brothers Karamazov* or *The Thousand and One Nights* or *The Magic Mountain*—is in some way less real than these same books after the historical excavator has done with them. He implies this because he regards an understanding of the relation of the book to its period and its society not only as a help in understanding it more fully, but as a first interpretative principle which, by explaining both the novel and our response to it in a new way, turns them into something else. The 'real' work is therefore not the one which originally convinced us because it was true to experience; nor was our conviction 'real'; both are as unreal as Mr. Eliot's religion. Mr. Daiches' insistence on this is merely another form of his insistence that the political interpretation is not merely one among several interpretations, but the only real one. What we gain by that interpretation is clearness—'rarely has the nature of the contemporary situation been so clear'. What we lose is the conviction that in a work of imagination a mind can speak to a mind, immediately.

A short note on such a controversial subject must necessarily simplify things which are not simple. But questions must be simple, and I have one more. The thesis which Mr. Daiches works out in his book is 'that the most serious and important section of modern fiction represents an attempted adjustment between literature and a certain state of transition in civilisation and culture generally, and that this adjustment explains most of the differentiating features of the twentieth-century novel as well as providing an impressive example of the kind of relation that exists and always has existed between any particular art and the general state of civilisation'. He also considers that the adjustment to the transition explains the many experiments in form and language which mark the period. That period produced in this country *Ulysses*, *Sons and Lovers*, *To the Lighthouse*, *Nightwood*, and on the continent the works of Proust, Thomas Mann and Franz Kafka. The writers of this century have certainly been troubled by the problem of an era of transition; but it is clear that they have also been troubled by the desire to convey a new sense of experience. To say this, of course, is not to get past Mr. Daiches, for he can reply that that new sense of experience can also be explained by the writer's adjustment to a state of transition. But it cannot be imaginatively understood on that hypothesis; it loses its own reality and takes on a different reality in which all that was individual in it is generalised. Adjustment is not an adequate term for the experience described by Proust in *Le Temps retrouvé*, which drove him to devote the rest of his life to the resuscitation within him of *the Eternal Man*. It cannot explain any individual work, but only behaviour in general. If we could see our time with the eyes of a future historian, we would realise that everyone living in it—not only the writer but the capitalist, the Communist, the grocer, the scientist, the criminal, the banker and the baker—is 'adjusted' to it in the most exact way. They have no choice. But that does not tell us much about them. The real defect of Mr. Daiches' interpretation of literature, and of other interpretations of the same kind, is not that they are untrue (there is a good deal of truth in them), but that they are inadequate.

THE DECLINE OF THE NOVEL

WHEN one tries to define the difference between the position of the novelist fifty or a hundred years ago and his position to-day one finds that, though far-reaching, it can be put in simple terms. To the novelist fifty or a hundred years ago life obediently fell into the mould of a story; to the novelist to-day it refuses to do so. This recalcitrance of the subject-matter is not absolute; the novelist still manages to tell a story: *Ulysses* is a story. But it is a story without an ending, and the characteristic modern novel is a story without an ending. At the start the novelist finds that his theme moulds itself obediently enough into a story, and the impetus carries him along for a while; but then it weakens, and when it has weakened to vanishing point the story has to stop, for it has no fixed destination. The modern novel is like a sentence that sets out confidently; the grammatical construction is ingenious; we admire the writer's skill in insinuating explanatory and qualifying clauses and all sorts of parentheses; but the sentence remains hanging in the air. This is another way of saying that the contemporary novelist has an imaginative grasp of origins but not of ends. There was a time when the novelist (and the poet and everybody) had a grasp of both. To have this is a mark of that order of thought and imagination which is generally called classical. Our own order is not a classical order; we have a grasp of origins but not of ends; our existence, like our works, is an unfinished sentence. And the novel describing the life we live is a symptom of the order in which we live; its incompleteness is a reflection of the incompleteness of a whole region of thought and belief.

This is obvious enough; but our position in time makes it difficult for us to acknowledge it. We look upon the contemporary novel as one thing, and the order out of which it springs as another, and regard their problems as separate problems. We do not make this mistake when we think of the eighteenth-century novel; for when we read Fielding or Sterne we are conscious of the general body of sentiment, belief and thought that went into their work and belonged to the eighteenth century and to no other. Standing outside the eighteenth century, we can see it whole. But we cannot stand outside our own century, for we are part of it, and so the contemporary novel is a special and technical problem to us, one among many problems. Yet really there is perhaps only the problem caused by the lack of a normal and complete order in which existence would have unity and meaning.

Before going further it would be best to show what I mean by a story with and without an ending:

(A) Joseph remains blest with his Fanny, whom he doats on with the utmost tenderness, which is all returned on her side. The happiness of this couple is a perpetual fountain of pleasure to their fond parents; and, what is particularly remarkable, he declares he will imitate them in their retirement, nor will he be prevailed on by any booksellers, or their authors, to make his appearance in high life.

(B) I lingered round them [the graves], under that benign sky: watched the moths fluttering among the heath and harebells, listened to the soft wind breathing through the grass, and wondered how anyone could ever imagine unquiet slumbers for the sleepers in that quiet earth.

(C) She ran forward, always forward, into a faint streak of light. The darkness unfolded before her. There was joy in the running and with every step she took she achieved a new sense of escape. A delicious notion came into her mind. As she ran she thought the light under her feet became more distinct. It was, she thought, as though the darkness had grown afraid of her presence and sprang aside, out of her path. There was a sensation of boldness. She had herself become something that within itself contained light. She was a creator of light. At her approach darkness grew afraid and fled away into the distance. When that thought came she found herself able to run without stopping to rest and half wished she might run on for ever, through the land, through towns and cities, driving darkness away with her presence.

(D) Quickly, as if she were recalled by something over there, she turned to her canvas. There it was—her picture. Yes, with all its greens and blues, its lines running up and across, its attempt at something. It would be hung in the attic, she thought; it would be destroyed. But what did that matter? she asked herself, taking up her brush again. She looked at the steps; they were empty; she looked at her canvas; it was blurred. With a sudden intensity, as if she saw it clear for a second, she drew a line there, in the centre. It was done; it was finished. Yes, she thought, laying down her brush in extreme fatigue, I have had my vision.

These four passages, in their order, are the last paragraphs of *Joseph Andrews*, *Wuthering Heights*, Sherwood Anderson's *Out of Nowhere into Nothing*, and Virginia Woolf's *To the Lighthouse*. The thing which strikes us most strongly now about the end of *Joseph Andrews* is its banality; indeed the end of the traditional novel, when it is not tragic as in *Wuthering Heights*, is generally banal, for it is expected. The last words in the stories by Sherwood Anderson and Virginia Woolf are far more interesting and more worthy of the mind's attention, for they show a deeper concern with the problem of experience, and can therefore be taken more seriously than Fielding's, which are purely conventional, a mere ceremonious good-bye to the chief characters. But though they are more interesting, and even significant, they are not entirely convincing; or rather they convince us only of the authors' search for a new kind of experience, not of the reality and ultimate significance of that experience as attributed to the characters. The significance of the traditional novel, whether comic like *Joseph Andrews*, or tragic like *Wuthering Heights*, lies within it, and the conclusion is merely a conclusion. In *Out of Nowhere into Nothing* and *To the Lighthouse*, the writer is still struggling to seize the full significance when the story ends. After Joseph is married and Heathcliff is buried, we feel there is nothing more to say. But after reading the last words of Sherwood Anderson and Virginia Woolf we feel that there is still something of the greatest importance to say, and that the ending is really a sort of beginning, the beginning of a quite different story. Something should have followed; but what that something is we do not know, because we live by an unfinished conception of life, exist in a circle which is never closed. Such endings are expressions of a hope of completion, arrows shot into the irresponsive future. Lawrence's *Sons and Lovers* ends with Paul striding back towards the lights of the town with his fists clenched; Joyce's *Portrait of the Artist as a Young Man*, with Stephen's solemn proclamation of his creed as a writer. Fifty or a hundred years ago a novelist would have asked: What next? What will happen when Paul is back in the town and has to unclench his fists? What will happen to Stephen's creed as a writer? Will it have changed in five or ten years' time? But our imagination stops short at a certain point and cannot go farther, for Paul and Stephen are launched into a world where neither their creators nor we can follow them. They stand at the beginning of a story which is never told.

A story without an ending describes a mode of existence which has not been thought out and stops short of meaning. The vision or the illumination is an acknowledgment of that lack of meaning, an attempt to fill up a void with a personal and mystical hope. A comprehensive and widely accepted conception of human life produces good imaginative art; a tentative and partially accepted conception of life, unsatisfactory imaginative art. In an age when such a conception prevails the subject-matter of the artist will not mould itself into a form; every image of human existence will have the mark of organic imperfection.

Is there any universal mark by which we can recognise a conception of human life that is complete and in a high sense normal to mankind? I shall hazard the assertion that all such conceptions postulate a transcendent reality and recognise man's relation to it, and that human life must always stop short of meaning if we seek its meaning merely in itself. To seek its meaning in itself is to seek its meaning in time; and the conception of life which prevails to-day is a conception of life purely in time. The contemporary novel is a story of time against a background of time. The traditional novel is a story of time against a permanent pattern. This does not mean that Fielding or Jane Austen were religious in any sense, or that when describing Tom Jones or Elizabeth Bennet they were concerned with eternal truths. But they lived in an order in which everybody possessed without thinking about it much the feeling for a permanence above the permanence of one human existence, and believed that the ceaseless flux of life passed against an unchangeable background. Men still felt this whether they were Christians or not. They felt also that there was a relation between the brief story of man and that unchangeable order; and this sentiment, in whatever terms it was held, was the final earnest of the completeness of their conception of life.

To return to the novel: it may be advanced that without

this permanent background there can be no whole picture of life. Seen against eternity the life of man is a complete story. Seen against time it is an unfinished one, a part of endless change, a fleeting picture on an unstable substance. The traditional recognition of a permanence beyond the duration of the happenings told in one story belongs to a certain mode of thinking and feeling which has prevailed during the known past of European civilisation; it now prevails effectually no longer. That mode was auspicious to imaginative literature; and originally it was the creation of religion. So that in a sense imaginative literature is, if not the child, at least the grandchild or great-grandchild of religion. It may be that in its early stages the decay of religion encourages the production of imaginative litera- ture, and the one thrives at the expense of the other, as during the Renaissance; but the complete decay of the religious sense would bring with it the atrophy of the creative imagination, which needs as a working hypothesis something more durable than the immediate subject- matter on which it works. It may be (if we can put reliance on contemporary theorists who think in terms of thousands of years, future years) that poetical and imaginative pro- duction is merely a passing human activity made possible by certain historical conditions and fated to disappear with them. This is the complement of another theory: that we are witnessing in our time the definitive liquidation of religion, and that in a few centuries the religious sense will have vanished for good. If that were so, it would be easy to believe that poetry and imagination in all its forms would disappear too. But the question is whether the religious sense can ever disappear. If it cannot, then neither can poetry and the various other forms of imaginative art.

The norm of human existence remains. There are cer- tain beliefs which are natural to man, for they satisfy his

mind and heart better than any alternative ones. The mark
of such beliefs is their completeness; they close the circle.
In a state of irremediable imperfection such as man's, the
circle can be closed only by calling on something beyond
man; by postulating a transcendent reality. So the belief
in eternity is natural to man; and all the arts, all the forms
of imaginative literature, since they depend on that belief,
are equally natural to him. When that belief partially fails,
imagination suffers an eclipse, and art becomes a problem
instead of a function. If that belief were to fail completely
and for good, there would be no imaginative art with a
significance beyond its own time. But it is inconceivable
that it should fail, for it is native to man.

THE NATURAL MAN AND THE
POLITICAL MAN

THE history of the modern novel describes the disappearance of man as religion and humanism conceived him. Instead, there has emerged a new species of the natural man dovetailed into a biological sequence and a social structure. This natural man is capable of betterment but, unlike the natural man of religion, has no need for regeneration. He is simply a human model capable of indefinite improvement on the natural plane; the improvement depending ultimately on the progress of society, and of things in general.

Towards the end of last century it was fashionable to call this new natural man 'the thinking animal', and he has since been called 'the unique animal'. He follows a natural development from birth to death, and since this is all that is allowed him, it is important that he should pass through all its stages—childhood, adolescence, love, maturity—in a manner closely corresponding to the requirements of nature; otherwise he will be 'frustrated' or 'distorted'. His upbringing, his surroundings, his ideas, should be as 'natural' as possible. If they are, the expectation is that he will turn out to be satisfactory.

But in practice it is discovered that he is never quite satisfactory, that some residue of frustration or distortion always remains in him. This residue is taken to be due to the imperfection of our political and social system, and under a perfect constitution the assumption is that it would disappear. The corollary of the natural man is consequently the political man: the man conscious that something must be done collectively by all natural men, or a majority or an effective minority of them, in order that an opportunity may be given to every natural man to develop his natural potentialities in the most natural way conceivable.

The difference between the man of myth and religion and the new natural man is quite simple. The first was not regarded as human in the complete sense until he put on the spiritual man; he had to be made anew by a process which did not enter into the rest of the biological sequence. This process was conceived symbolically as a rebirth, a spiritual act by which man was integrated into his true image and became conscious of his unique place in the world and in time. We may conceive the spiritual man as being grafted on the natural man, or as being innate in him and seeking to emerge from him into complete humanity. In either case, as the new man can exist only in the body of the old, his co-existence with the old implies a moral struggle in the centre of the individual, a struggle which determines in all sorts of ways his struggle to adapt himself to society, or society to himself, but is different in its intimacy, its unavoidability and its apparent lack of utilitarian causation. This fundamental moral struggle within the individual was for many centuries accepted as the essential character of man. This being suspended between good and evil by a law inherent in his nature is the man of Dante and Shakespeare, and of Balzac and Tolstoy. He occupies a country of his own with unique rights and needs, quite apart from the biological sequence.

During a number of generations the frontiers of that country have been crumbling away. For the separate autonomous drama of mankind we have gradually substituted a natural process. The result has been a reduction of the image of man, who has become simpler, more temporal, more realistic and more insignificant.

The difference between man as he was conceived by Christian theology, by Dante, Milton, Pascal and the tragic poets of England and France in the sixteenth and seventeenth centuries, and man as he is understood in different ways by H. G. Wells, the early Aldous Huxley, Mr. Ernest Hemingway, M. Henri de Montherlant and a great number of popular middle-brow novelists—for the most important point about the new conception is that it has become the popular conception—is difficult to define, though obviously great. One way of expressing it is by saying that to the traditional man the individual's life was a conflict, and that to the modern man it is a development. The conflict has been stated in various terms; but the formulation of it which is closest to our own ways of thinking and most readily understandable by us is that which we find in Milton and Racine: the conflict is a conflict between reason and passion or impulse. This formula was accepted as valid throughout the seventeenth and also a great part of the eighteenth century, though in its later stages in a somewhat mechanical way; reason and impulse tending to become categories instead of vital principles.

The Romantic Movement reinstated impulse, but it also did something else; it tended to identify reason with impulse; it substituted for the old conflict a sort of mystical co-operation. France, with its capacity for stating everything rationally, first worked out the implications of the new attitude. By a succession of writers from Madame de Staël to George Sand and Alfred de Musset the impulses were declared to be sacred, and more reasonable than reason itself. This phase, strewn with the wrecks of spontaneous love affairs, and illustrated by a confused crowd of anonymous Byrons and Chateaubriands, did not last for very long. But it left behind, in spite of failure in practice, the assumption that reason and impulse worked in co-operation; and if this was so, there was nothing left for the individual but to develop. This assumption was merely implicit in the work of the romantics; it was not formulated until much later. It required for its formulation certain theories drawn from Darwin, and particularly the idea of evolution applied to the life of the individual. The old conflict was gone, or was hidden away. Darwin and the orthodox economists taught man the necessity for adaptation; Spencer and the Utopians opened before him the endless possibilities of evolution. The adaptation was a present need; the evolution, a future contingency. But at the same time the adaptation was a changing adaptation, for the environment of man was changing, and therefore to adapt oneself was to evolve. That the evolution might have no moral principle, that the environment of man might change for the worse instead of for the better, was not seriously considered.

To contemplate man's image of himself changing and catch the stages of the change is almost as difficult as to imagine visually the process by which the countless animal species developed from a few simple prototypes. The idea of man current at any one time is not a homogeneous one; old conceptions linger on; new ones tentatively appear. The idea that man's life is a development, and part of a greater development which is essentially political or sociological, not moral or religious, was bound to lead to the conclusion that this development could be controlled, and that human life could be conditioned to a great extent, given the power and the equipment. To-day we can see this theory being applied on a large scale in several countries. For this theory man becomes a subject who responds in a more or less calculable way to certain things such as encouragement, suggestion, the carefully thought-out system which is called propaganda, intimidation, display, rubber truncheons and in general all the varieties of greed and hope and fear. As man is a creature with a natural development, entirely contained in his environment, all that is needed is to decide the terms within which he shall develop. Once these are settled by a sufficiently powerful group, men can be used with calculable accuracy.

This is a theory which could have been founded only on the new natural man developing within an environment in a calculable way, without any effective inward struggle, or any permanent conception of a desirable life, or any personal striving to realise it. If the theory does admit that such obstacles to its working exist it regards them as foolish, since they ignore the reality of *things*; such things as the power of the state, tanks, shells, concentration camps, and such things also as the natural man's appetites, vanities, angers, hopes, fears and hatreds, which can always be aroused, and which, with a little direction, can become irresistible. Consequently what has gradually been brought into prominence by the religion of development is the primacy of *things*, and it finds its fulfilment in the theory that men can be conditioned by things. Control things and you control mankind. In this conception the moral struggle which possessed the imagination of other ages, and was strong even a century ago, recedes into irrelevance, and becomes like one of those vestigial organs in the body which no longer perform any useful function, but exist merely to plague us: a sort of vermiform appendix.

It is easy to note the reduction of the image of man in contemporary politics, for there it presents itself in flesh and blood and works out logically in contempt for human

freedom and for human life, things which always go together. To see it in contemporary literature is more difficult. Perhaps it can be best seen in a drastic simplicity.
In his book *Modernes*, M. Denis Saurat makes the generalisation that in French literature the classical writers of the
seventeenth century exalted reason, the Romantics of the
nineteenth century emotion, and certain contemporary
writers sensation. This generalisation traces the graph of
the modern fall of man. It is a descent from complexity to
simplicity, from the civilised to the primitive.

An idea of the change in our attitude to human life
may be had by comparing any character in Dickens with
any character in the early work of Mr. Ernest Hemingway. Dickens was an emotional writer, but he still knew
that there was in the individual a struggle between impulse and reason. He was not a religious writer, but his
characters still lived on a plane which was partly spiritual
and partly natural. Mr. Hemingway's early characters
live on the natural plane alone. The two gunmen in his
short story, *The Killers*, are mechanical murderers, and
their victim a mechanical murderee; they are all equally
conditioned; and there is nothing to be said about them,
except that they evoke the kind of pity and horror one
might feel in watching some hunting beast pulling down
and killing its prey. The story is astonishingly natural
from one point of view, and astonishingly unnatural from
another; for after all the characters are not animals but
merely men thinking and feeling and acting in an extraordinarily circumscribed way. The murderers have no
remorse; the victim has no feeling except animal resignation. The immediate lust to kill, the immediate dread of
being killed, are all that remain. There is nothing but
sensation.

Turn from this to Dickens. Jonas Chuzzlewit too is a

murderer, but he never suggests to our minds the picture of an animal armed with a gun or a knife; he remains a human being with thoughts and emotions, horrible enough, certainly, yet drawn from the general source of human thought and emotion. In his short story Mr. Hemingway is sure of only one thing, the immediate sensation, and, being a scrupulously honest writer, he confines himself to that and leaves out thought and emotion as much as possible. He starts with the natural man following his needs, suffering from his frustrations as a wounded animal might suffer. And starting from that, it was impossible for him to reach the world of emotions and thoughts, for they are a legacy from the traditional man and are determined by beliefs which assume that man is not natural in the same sense as an adder or an ape is natural.

Mr. Hemingway began to write in the years of disillusion which followed the 1914–18 war, and the man he describes is therefore the frustrated natural man. Probably no one else has described more vividly the horror of the natural man's life when he is driven and goaded and denied natural satisfaction, and retires into himself to lick his wounds, or seeks forgetfulness in drink or sex. For many years Mr. Hemingway went on describing the frustrated natural man, articulate only in violence or in sensual experience. Then he discovered that the frustrated natural man was not enough, but that he must transcend himself and become the political man. This was the discovery of a whole generation, not of Mr. Hemingway alone; what makes it particularly interesting in his case is that we can see it taking place in his work. He began with the undirected revolt of *Fiesta*; he attained the disciplined revolt of *For Whom the Bell Tolls*, with its glorification of the republican struggle in Spain. The man Mr. Hemingway describes in this book is still the natural man, fighting and lusting. He has merely added a few words to his vocabulary: the words liberty, fraternity and equality. They are sufficient in themselves to give him an aim beyond his appetites; but his way to them is still the way of the natural man; and only by fighting and killing can he achieve a world where there will be nothing to hinder his natural development, no obstacle, no frustration. The goal of all men has miraculously risen before him; although he has acknowledged nothing but sensation, three ideas have announced themselves to him; but they are in a different world from his world, and can be reached only in a different way from his way. They can be reached only by thought and feeling and the action which follows from them, while all that he can offer is sensation, a sort of *appetite* for liberty, equality and fraternity which drives him to batter down all that stands between him and them without knowing that, even if he were to gain them, he could not, as he is, enjoy them. This incompatibility between the natural man and his political aims makes Mr. Hemingway's later work sentimental in a curious way; it is as if we saw Caliban looking through the eyes of Prospero, and, without Prospero's rod, swearing to perform Prospero's miracle with his naked fists. This sentimentality of violence is implicit in the work of all writers who conceive Utopia as a kingdom to be taken by storm. Mr. Hemingway's first frustrated men were far more real.

The frustrated natural man was a popular, almost a typical, figure in the novel after the 1914–18 war, when hope and belief were at their lowest ebb. Some of the writers who wrote about him then have since given him up and turned elsewhere for a more adequate conception; Mr. Aldous Huxley, for example. But those who stuck to him and tried to educe something positive from him were finally left with no choice but to turn him into the political man. And when the natural man becomes political, there seem to be only two directions in which he can advance: towards Communism or towards Fascism. The man who thinks of himself as developing within an environment, without any deep-rooted resistance, will ultimately prefer that the terms of his environment should be laid down unmistakably, so that a clear channel may be provided for his impulses. In following these impulses he knows the only kind of freedom which he can know; and as that freedom seems infinitely dear to him in prospect, he is prepared even to die for it. Communism and Fascism, which both believe in the natural man, provide a channel for his impulses, in the one case a channel which may lead him to live better, in the other a steep road rushing steadily downwards, where he will bury himself entirely in nature in a sort of sacred frenzy. When the inward struggle of the individual is regarded as irrelevant such things as these can be achieved; the one thing which cannot be achieved is liberty.

Communism, by postulating the natural man and using him as he is, with his needs and his desires, tries to teach him; there are religious implications in Communism, no matter how carefully Communists may rule them out. Fascism is far more radically involved with the natural man, and rests upon him entirely. It does not look beyond him, but glorifies him, sees in him the sole hope of the future, and regards the spirit, the intellect and the rarer uses of the senses merely as diseases marring his natural perfection. The two modern writers who have described the natural man most penetratingly and eloquently are D. H. Lawrence and Henri de Montherlant, and Lawrence is a great writer. They are not pre-eminently political in their attitude. In Lawrence we have a fierce exposure of the squalor of our industrial civilisation, and in Monther-

lant a contempt for all the shams of the age and a ruthless
assertion of the right of the natural man to go his own way.
They both criticise society from the 'natural' point of
view. Lawrence's criticism of Industrialism is that it frustrates even the simplest natural impulses, and sex in particular, the central impulse: the criticism is valuable because it is fundamental. Against the synthetic monstrosity
of modern life he sets the values of blood and soil, the
first natural values, essential because natural. But having
affirmed them, he turns against what he calls 'the white
consciousness', the bloodless consciousness of the spirit;
and whether he does this because it is spirit or because it
is diseased spirit it is impossible to say. He preferred the
primitive, for he felt that only the primitive, in a world he
hated so much, was still sound. He was outraged by the
Christian counsel to love your neighbour, and retorted
that hate was often more honest and salutary; for hate was
an instinctive discharge of energy, and in a world which
lived mainly by routine, any instinctive discharge was to
him its own justification. He asserted all the impulses of
the natural man, love, hatred, anger, cruelty, and found
a mystical meaning in the working of the passions. He
wanted mankind to start again at the beginning, in a state
beyond good and evil, and never reach the Fall. He would
have been satisfied if man could be born properly once.
The question is whether man can be born properly once,
and therefore whether Lawrence's gospel was a dream. He
saw that our senses and impulses were frustrated at every
point by the life we live; he wanted a state in which they
would function naturally, without distortion. He saw that
such a state would be better than our present one. He
believed that this state could be reached by a sort of
mystical assertion of the natural man; here he forestalled
the Nazis. But the Nazis themselves have shown to what

a belief of this kind leads; to violence, persecution, cruelty, war and, in the last resort, slavery. For the natural man is violent, quarrelsome, greedy, and also, since he has no permanent inner resistance, bound to be enslaved.

Montherlant's picture of the natural man is more sophisticated. His natural man has attended fashionable parties, and knows all the tricks of the social life. At the same time he has the greatest contempt for society and is by conviction anti-social. He is much more formidable than Lawrence's natural man; for he has examined the life of the spirit and sardonically dismissed it. He scorns the world in which he lives, a world of dupes; but he has no wish to change it; he is content that he himself should live the infinitely preferable life of an unusually honest and vital natural man. He is exclusive; he insists on his privileges. If he has a counterpart in the Fascist hierarchy, it is among the leaders who use the beliefs of the ordinary man for their own purposes, and see through the mythology while exploiting it.

The importance of Lawrence and Montherlant is that they draw with exceptional honesty the consequences of a belief in the natural man. These consequences are very different from those which his original sponsors expected. The believers in evolution thought that the natural man contained within himself endless potentialities of improvement; and their faith was founded on a mystical belief in the necessary tendency of things to go on improving for all time; it was founded on a faith in things. Man had merely to develop; and his development was guaranteed by the beneficial development of things, which was certain. Then it was discovered that man was not a single term in the equation, that some were fitted to lay down, within the human sphere, the conditions on which man should develop, and that others were fitted only to observe those conditions. For the first was reserved the actual conduct of human policy; for the second, a mythology that would please or inspire them, and make them eager to obey and ready to lay down their lives. Human life thus became a thing completely contained in an environment, and therefore a thing to which the imagination could give no ultimate significance, since there was not in it even the pretence of choice, even the day-dream of freedom. If the life of the individual is a development, then that development is simple and inevitable. If the life of the individual is a conflict, then that conflict implies a choice, and the choice, uncertainty, and uncertainty, the existence of more in human life than can be compressed into a formula. What has taken place in literature is a simplification of the idea of man, connected with this notion of natural process and development. The simplification is a general tendency; literature has not initiated but merely reflected it; and only those writers who are deeply rooted in tradition, and possessed with the idea of time, have been able to make headway against it; such writers as Proust, James Joyce and Virginia Woolf, to confine ourselves to the novelists: there are similar figures in poetry. The obsession of such writers with tradition was called out by this human crisis. But Lawrence, Hemingway and Montherlant are completely in the modern convention. They accept the new leaf which history has turned, the leaf on which the war was written. They themselves write on that leaf, and the first words written on a new leaf, even by genius, are never new but merely primitive, a repetition or a variation of words written on the first leaf of all, before civilisation began.

And yet history and experience tell us that human life is a development, not merely a struggle poised on its own centre, changing nothing. The struggle is an essential means for accomplishing the development. The evolutionists seemed to acknowledge this in their nineteenth-century formulas—the struggle for existence, the survival of the fittest, the adaptation to environment. Where they went wrong was in misconceiving the nature of the struggle. They regarded it merely as a function of the development and nothing more; 'the struggle for existence', 'adaptation to environment', meant only this. And if we regard the struggle merely as a function of development we create a mechanical universe with which the living mind can do nothing, since we eliminate the individual in whom alone the struggle attains self-consciousness, and rob development of all moral significance by substituting for the attainment of aims which men strive for because they are good, the mere accomplishment of a general process. Socialism and Communism are moral ideas, and spring from the desire to establish brotherhood and justice; without that desire they could never have arisen, and lacking it they are bound to accomplish something different from their proper end. For as man is a moral being, human development can be conceived only as a moral development; no evolutionary process can bring us brotherhood and justice, for they are not things merely to be ratified in a code (though a code is necessary), but principles to be given reality in all our private and public relations throughout society.

There is then a development, though it is not that which was formulated by the nineteenth-century evolutionists. And there is also a co-operation between reason and impulse, though it is not that which was embraced by Byron and George Sand. Without it indeed society would remain a hypothesis permanently beyond realisation. In exalting impulse, then, the Romantics did something which had to be done. The sedate see-saw of the eighteenth century with its mechanical opposition of reason and impulse, of man and nature, now one up, now the other, could not last. Pope, in presuming not God to scan and declaring that the proper study of mankind was man, enclosed man in an elegant vacuum, cut him off from nature in which his roots were fastened, and from God in whom he had his being. Man, God and nature were stationed at a neat Newtonian distance from one another; and this could be done with the complete approval of the mind because all three had become abstractions. To Wordsworth, on the other hand, musing

> *On Man, on Nature, and on Human Life,*

these three entities interpenetrated one another in innumerable ways; nature was to him a 'mighty sum of things for ever speaking', and God pervaded nature, so that there could be seen in

> *the sick sight*
> *And giddy prospect of the raving stream,*
> *The unfettered clouds and region of the Heavens,*

the

> *workings of one mind, the features*
> *Of the same face, blossoms upon one tree;*
> *Characters of the great Apocalypse,*
> *The types and symbols of Eternity,*
> *Of first, and last, and midst, and without end.*

In *The Prelude* it was Wordsworth's main object to show

> *How exquisitely the individual Mind*
> *(And the progressive powers perhaps no less*
> *Of the whole species) to the external World*
> *Is fitted:—and how exquisitely, too—*
> *Theme this but little heard of among men—*
> *The external World is fitted to the Mind;*
> *And the creation (by no lower name*
> *Can it be called) which they with blended might*
> *Accomplish:—this is our high argument.*

The poetry of Wordsworth has the truth of a vision—
the vision he saw as a child and in two periods of his
young manhood. To seize its truth in experience an unusual exercise of discrimination is needed. For it records
a moment of mystical co-operation between reason and
impulse, man and nature; it does not describe a process, or
make a general statement about life which can be embodied in a theory. It is rather the outline of a possibility,
and the record of moments in which that possibility was
realised. But Wordsworth's followers vulgarised his conception of nature, and reduced to a dogma what to him
had been an illumination; and between them with their
crude faith in mountains and woods and the evolutionists
with their benevolent universe evolving towards even
greater benevolence, there was an intellectual and emotional affinity. Both of them, unintentionally, helped to set
the moving principle of good outside man, and in doing
so helped to dehumanise experience and history; whereas
Wordsworth was essentially concerned with the mind of
man and its capacity to respond to the mighty sum of
things for ever speaking. In the response lay the co-operation between impulse and reason, and the possibility of
harmony; without the response there was no harmony, and
it could not be created by means of a theory concerning it.
But the theory, nevertheless, dominated the nineteenth
century, and has extended its influence over ours.

III

PANURGE AND FALSTAFF

THESE two characters occupy a curiously similar position in the groups enclosing them. Falstaff is the friend and butt of Prince Hal, the heir to the crown, with the King in the background. Panurge occupies a similar position towards Pantagruel, who is also the heir to the crown, with Gargantua, the King his father, now and then benevolently appearing. Both heroes are members of a fellowship; both are drinkers, and fond of company; both are promiscuous lovers and flouters of the law. At the outset we see Falstaff preparing to bring off a robbery at Gadshill; and we are introduced to Panurge in these words:

> He was at that time five and thirty years old or thereabouts, fine to gild like a leaden dagger; for he was a notable cheater and cony-catcher, he was a very gallant and proper man of his person, only that he was a little lecherous, and naturally subject to a kind of disease, which at that time they called lack of money: it is an incomparable grief, yet, notwithstanding he had three-score and three tricks to come by it to his need, of which the most honourable and most ordinary was in manner of thieving, secret purloining and filching; for he was a wicked lewd rogue, a cosener, drinker, royster, rover, and a very dissolute and debauched fellow, if there were any in Paris; otherwise, and in all matters else, the best and most vertuous man in the world; and he was still contriving some plot, and devising mischief against the Sergeants and the watch.

Apply that description to Falstaff, and except for age it fits him. The two men belong to the same world; they might easily have belonged to the same fellowship.

But they end very differently. Falstaff dies of a broken

heart, while Panurge reaches the Temple of the Holy Bottle and the noble priestess Bacbac reveals to him the word that solves all his difficulties and ends all his cares. Behind these two conclusions we feel clearly the difference between the imaginative intention of Rabelais and of Shakespeare, and more obscurely we can guess at a difference between the French and the English attitude to certain things, and especially to the life of the appetites and the senses. Take deep drinking, which may stand symbolically for the philosophy both of Falstaff and Panurge. In Shakespeare it is enjoyed aesthetically as an excess of nature; while in Rabelais it is given a moral foundation, and regarded as a rare and precious natural gift out of which the utmost good must be got by civilising it. Falstaff, one feels, is in some ways the worse, but Panurge, and the admirable and benevolent Pantagruel, are always the better, for their drinking. To say this is to speak symbolically, as Rabelais himself did. What I want to suggest is that the French have managed to weave into the pattern of civilised life a greater number of unpromising and excessive factors than the English have, or rather to acclimatise in their atmosphere more of the natural powers of human nature, neither good nor bad in themselves, and turn them to use and to virtue. They include more of nature in their scheme of civilised behaviour, and make a more kindly allowance for it; but without compromising their intellectual and spiritual honesty.

Rabelais' book is the first and chief instance of this kindly and hospitable operation of the French spirit. Rabelais is a great moralist, and just as great when he is carried away in an excess of sculduggery or bawdiness as when he is writing about the highest mysteries. Reading him perceptively we are astonished over and over again by his almost infallible sense of rightness, an extravagant sanity. He is one of those writers who can admire the best without thinking less of the good, and praise the good unstintingly without doubting that there is something better. He praises everything in its place, and there is hardly anything natural in which he does not find matter for praise; but his praise is never indiscriminate, like Whitman's, or falsely mystical; Whitman's eulogy of the cow because it does not lie in bed at night and weep for its sins would have entertained him vastly, or have shocked him, for he still lived in a world where men and cows knew their places. He found the spiritual man good: he also found the natural man good. He had no doubt which of them was the better, but his admiration for the one did not provide him with the least temptation to look down on the other. This is the reason for the impression of paradox which he gives us; but it is the unavoidable, the necessary paradox. There is not a trace of superciliousness in him; even his satire has only a mock ferocity; it is beneath him to make a point against anyone; he leaves that to laughter, and when it comes everything is carried away on it, himself as well as the abuses he is reforming. Or rather the mere magnificence of his generosity and universality of his acceptance of things reduces these ills and makes them dwindle into an insectlike quaintness and absurdity. His satire is like no other satire, for one can hardly say that there is indignation in it, but rather surprise and half-shocked, half-delighted incredulity. Incredulity was one of his sharpest weapons, if one can attribute sharpness to such a sanguine and cordial spirit.

It is the completeness of his acceptance of things which accounts for what is called his Rabelaisianism and justifies it: in accepting life he could not baulk at the human body and its functions and humours; he would have been halted, in that case, at the very threshold of his undertaking. He takes this obstacle boldly, the only way in which it can be taken without offence. In doing this he can occasionally be brutal, but only with the brutality of his age, as Shakespeare was; and he never offends our moral sense so deeply as Shakespeare does when at the battle of Shrewsbury he makes Falstaff gash the dead body of Hotspur and pretend that he has killed him, and the Prince complaisantly enters into the plot against the good fame of a brave enemy. The torrential humour of Rabelais, in which he catches up all that man is in his prepared and unprepared moments, is more frank and free, more rough and ready, than Shakespeare's; but it treats goodness with the most tender regard; and when he has laughed away false delicacy, he sometimes shows a delicacy rare for his time. But he had to laugh away the false delicacy, for he was consumed with the desire to accept things as they are.

This desire to accept all things has, like everything in Rabelais, two faces; it is wild and excessive, being absolute; and it is ultimately sane, being a plain human necessity. This is why drink, in which there is intoxication, and in which there is truth, occupies such a great part of his book, both actually and symbolically, from the moment when Gargantua is born crying, 'Some drink, some drink, some drink', till the moment when Panurge is led to the Temple of the Holy Bottle and the mystical word, 'Trinc' is uttered to him. The perennial thirst for wine becomes the symbol of a thirst for all things:

Which was first; thirst or drinking? Thirst, for who in the time of innocence would have drunk without being athirst? . . . I never drink without thirst, either present or future, to prevent it; as you know, I drink for the thirst to come; I drink eternally, this is to me an eternity of drinking, and drinking of eternity; let us sing, let us drink, and tune up our round-lays. Basta, enough, I sup, I wet, I humect, I moisten my gullet, I drink, and all for fear of dying; drink always and you shall never die: if I drink not, I am a ground dry, gravelled and spent, I am stark dead without drink, and my soul ready to fly into some marish amongst Frogs; the soul never dwells in a dry place, drouth kills it.

This is an image of Rabelais' thirst for all things; it is wild and excessive, but it is made sane, and becomes the formula for a universal truth about life, by the complete frankness with which it is given utterance. In listening to these extravagances we sometimes feel we are listening to an oracle.

But to understand the spirit in which Rabelais sets Panurge and Gargantua and Pantagruel before us, we have to turn to other passages where he expresses himself in a more elevated style. The speech by Friar John of the Funnels is in his middle style, which can be magnificent:

And lustie my lads, some bousing liquor, Page! O how good is God that gives us of this excellent juice! I call him to witness, if I had been in the time of Jesus Christ, I would have kept him from being taken by the Jews in the Garden of Olivet; and the the devil fail me, if I should have failed to cut off the hams of these gentlemen Apostles, who ran away so basely after they had well supped, and left their good Master in the lurch. I hate that man worse than poison that offers to run away, when he should fight and lay stoutly about him.

Rabelais is more completely himself in 'Panurge's Excuse and Exposition of the Monastic Mystery Concerning Powder'd Beef':

Fy; not to sup at all, that is the Devil. Come Friar John, let us go break our fast; for if I hit on such a round Refection in the morning, as will serve throughly to fill the Mill-hopper and Hogshide of my Stomach, and furnish it with Meat and Drink sufficient, then at a pinch, as in the case of some extreme necessity which presseth, I could make a shift that day to forbear Dining. But not to Sup: A Plague rot that base Custom, which is an error offensive to Nature. That Lady made the Day for exercise, to travel, work, wait on and labour in each his Negotiation and

Employment; and that we may with the more Fervency and Ardour prosecute our business, she sets before us a clear burning Candle, to wit, the Sun's resplendency: And at Night, when she begins to take the Light from us, she thereby tacitly implies no less, than if she would have spoken thus to us: My Lads and Lasses, all of you are good and honest folks, you have wrought well to-day, toiled and turmoiled enough, the Night approacheth, therefore cast off these moiling Cares of yours, desist from all your swinking painful labours, and set your minds how to refresh your bodies in the renewing of their vigour with good Bread, choice Wine, and store of wholesome Meats; then may you take some Sport and Recreation, and after that lie down and rest yourselves, that you may strongly, nimbly, lustily, and with the more alacrity to-morrow attend on your affairs as formerly.

This picture is thrown up by Panurge in the course of an argument against the custom of fasting; it is a modest image of Rabelais' ideal of human life. For a more complete and exalted notion of it we have to go to the account of Gargantua's education, and to the description of the Abbey of Thelema, where all freely come and go, where the men are free, well-born, well-bred, and conversant in honest companies, and 'never were seen Ladies so proper and handsome, so miniard and dainty, less froward, or more ready with their hand, and with their needle, in every honest and free action belonging to that sex', and where finally 'in all their rule, the strictest tie of their order, there was but this one clause to be observed, Do What Thou Wilt'. For, Rabelais says, men and women of such a kind 'have naturally an instinct and spur that prompteth them unto vertuous actions, and withdraws them from vice, which is called honour'.

It is this large spirit that animates the good-fellowship of Pantagruel and Panurge and Friar John and the others. Compared with the good-fellowship of Falstaff and his friends it is more cordial, gentle, and full of tender consideration. Panurge, like Falstaff, may be regarded as the butt of the company, but how gently he is teased, with what patience and consideration, so that his dignity as a human being is never offended. The epic sequence of discussions on the subject, Should Panurge marry, and if he married would he become a cuckold? is managed with a humorous solicitude for which there is no parallel in the rest of literature.

In this combination of frankness with consideration, the fellowship of Panurge is very unlike that of Falstaff. A spirit of warm geniality pervades the whole company of well-wishers. There is no shadow of envy, no touch of ill-nature. But if we turn to the fellowship at the Boar's Head Tavern, we find quite a different picture; all the geniality is provided by Falstaff himself, helped now and then by that neglected woman, Mistress Quickly. Prince Hal and his hanger-on, Poins, are never quite of the company; they are supercilious observers, prepared to involve themselves to a certain length, but no farther, for the entertainment they will get out of it. They have no consideration for Falstaff's dignity, or such dignity as he might have; they do all they can, rather ill-naturedly, to bring him to shame; they have towards him a sort of appreciative fondness, certainly, but that is all. From the start the Prince feels that he is lowering his dignity in associating with such company, and contrives an excuse to bolster it up:

> I know you all, and will a while uphold
> The unyoked humour of your idleness:
> Yet herein will I imitate the sun,
> Who doth permit the base contagious clouds
> To smother up his beauty from the world,
> That, when he please again to be himself,
> Being wanted, he may be more wonder'd at,
> By breaking through the foul and ugly mists
> Of vapours that did seem to strangle him.

The little crack was here, at the beginning, which was bound to break the fellowship and Falstaff's heart.

Falstaff is a far greater character than any of the figures in Rabelais' book. He is at the same time, in spite of the feeling of size that he gives us, a character spoilt in the making. We still seek an explanation for him, as we do for Hamlet; there are inconsistencies, or apparent inconsistencies, in him. The most obvious of these is between the emotion which he awakens in us, which is one of affection, and our knowledge of the things he has done. We see him robbing harmless merchants at Gadshill, pretending he is dead on the field of Shrewsbury to save his life, stabbing the dead body of Hotspur and claiming to have slain him. Yet these things do not seem to matter, except his treatment of Hotspur, in which he suddenly becomes repulsive. How can we like, approve, be enchanted by a man who does these things? We feel about Falstaff in this way because we think of him as living in a world of his own somewhat like the world of the Restoration comedy as Charles Lamb saw it, a world of play, apart from the world of responsibility: therefore not to be judged by moral standards. In his self-excusatory monologue Prince Hal says:

> *If all the year were playing holidays,*
> *To sport would be as tedious as to work;*
> *But when they seldom come, they wish'd for come,*
> *And nothing pleaseth but rare accidents.*

The year of playing holidays is the world in which Falstaff lives, and to which the Prince pays an occasional visit. But that world and the world of warring interests and political realities come closer and closer as the Prince draws nearer the throne, from which there are no holidays. What began as play becomes earnest; and for this the Prince, from start to finish, is responsible. If he had not

been so pleased with the rare accident of joining in rob-
beries, Falstaff might have continued his year of playing
holidays for a while longer. Yet apart from this, we feel
that the play world and the real world should not coalesce
in this way; and our imagination will always be outraged
by the scene where the newly crowned king disowns his
old companion. We feel as if something more valuable than
any throne were being disowned, as if fact were turning
upon imagination and pronouncing its foregone verdict
upon it.

Falstaff's world at the beginning, is a world of play in
which there is no discredit but merely enjoyment in robbing convenient merchants. He stands in much the same
relation to the serious set of characters as Bottom and his
friends to the lovers in *A Midsummer Night's Dream*. But
he is gradually forced out of the world of play into the
world of political necessity and contending interests, and
has to exchange one kind of reality for another. In the
course of this his original world is shown up in more
and more sordid colours, as it is submitted to a new and
exclusively practical criterion of judgment. The first part
of *Henry IV* begins with the words:

So shaken as we are, so wan with care,

spoken by the most uninteresting king that Shakespeare
ever drew. In this world wan with care, Falstaff is more
and more deeply involved, until we see him at last through
its eyes. The scenes on the field of Shrewsbury give the
first shock to our conception of him, and the recruiting
scene in Gloucester the second. As the Prince draws
nearer the throne, there is a violent change in the aspect
of Falstaff's old companions; we have a feeling that all the
lights are growing dirty and dim. New figures appear,
Doll Tearsheet and Pistol, figures of the underworld; and

Mistress Quickly, the respectable gossip, is suddenly revealed as the keeper of a bawdy house. Falstaff still retains some of his original splendour, but his companions become, after his death, mere commonplace rogues with no wit in them; Nym and Bardolf are hanged for stealing, Mistress Quickly dies in the spital, and Pistol is left reflecting:

> *Well, bawd I'll turn,*
> *And something lean to cutpurse of quick hand.*

That is how Falstaff's world of play ends. We feel this is not how it should end, or how Shakespeare would have liked it to end. We feel this most intensely in the epitaph on Falstaff which he puts in Mistress Quickly's mouth:

> A' made a finer end and went away an it had been any christom child; a' parted even just between twelve and one, even at the turning o' the tide: for after I saw him fumble with the sheets, and play with flowers, and smile upon his fingers' ends, I knew there was but one way; for his nose was as sharp as a pen, and a' babbled of green fields. 'How now, Sir John!' quoth I: 'what man! be o' good cheer.' So a' cried out, 'God, God, God!' three or four times. Now I, to comfort him, bid him a' should not think of God; I hoped there was no need to trouble himself with any such thoughts yet.

Mr. Middleton Murry says of Falstaff that he 'lives in and by a certain inimitable opulence of language'. Another way of putting this would be to say that he lives by a certain kind of talk which makes us feel that talk is endless because it is endlessly delightful. In the play this sense of endlessness comes from him alone; the other characters are gathered into it, but he is its only source, for as he himself says: 'I am not only witty in myself, but the cause that wit is in other men'. A few other figures in literature have the power to create this illusion of good talk that takes its ease and never comes to an end: Socrates, Panurge and Pantagruel, Mr. Shandy. In thinking of

them we have a picture of a company of friends sitting
round a table, in a tavern or a house, where there is meat
and drink; these are essential, for without them the cere-
mony would be without the symbolic character which is
immemorially associated with the breaking of bread together. Rabelais can spend a volume in creating this
curious kind of eternity, but Shakespeare has to do it in a
few scenes, interrupted by the incidents he had to invent
to keep the attention of a theatrical audience. He can do
this, in spite of these handicaps, because the impression
that talk is endless is not produced by its length. The
tricks which the Prince and Poins play on Falstaff are of
no interest except for the talk they provoke; and anything
else would have done as well. Our image of him, when we
try to call it up, is of a goodly, portly man and a corpulent
sitting with his friends in the Boar's Head Tavern, drinking and talking for ever; the rest of him is only intended
for the stage. To talk is his passion, and the fulfilment of
his nature:

> Hostess, clap to the doors: watch to-night, pray to-morrow.
> Gallants, lads, boys, hearts of gold, all the titles of good fellowship
> come to you. What, shall we be merry?

No one else of his company says that; for no one else had
his secret.

A curious thing about Falstaff, showing his primacy
over those who made game of him, is that the image of
him which stays in our minds is his own image, not that
of his observers; as if he alone were capable of describing
himself.

> Go thy ways, old Jack; die when thou wilt, if manhood, good
> manhood, be not forgot upon the face of the earth, then I am a
> shotten herring. There lives not three good men unhanged in
> England; and one of them is fat, and grows old.
> A goodly portly man, i' faith, and a corpulent; of a cheerful

look, a pleasing eye, and a most noble carriage; and, as I think, his age some fifty, or by'r lady, inclining to three score; and now I remember me, his name is Falstaff: if that man should be lewdly given, he deceiveth me; for, Harry, I see virtue in his looks.

The Prince's attempts to describe him, filled though they are with brilliant comparisons, are quite shallow, for he sees him from the outside, almost with a professional eye, as a performing buffoon. When Falstaff asks him the time of day, he replies:

What a devil hast thou to do with the time of day? Unless hours were cups of sack, and minutes capons, and clocks the tongues of bawds, and dials the signs of leaping-houses, and the blessed sun himself a fair hot wench in flame-coloured taffeta, I see no reason why thou shouldst be so superfluous to demand the time of the day.

A wonderful half-legendary vision of Falstaff, but an external one.

The most memorable descriptions of Falstaff, apart from his own, come from Mistress Quickly, who had more of his large kindliness of nature than any of his other companions:

Thou didst swear to me upon a parcel-gilt goblet, sitting in my Dolphin chamber, at the round table, at a sea-coal fire, upon Wednesday in Wheeson week, when the prince broke thy head for liking his father to a singing man of Windsor, thou didst swear to me then, as I was washing thy wound, to marry me and make me my lady thy wife. Canst thou deny it? Did not good-wife, Keech, the butcher's wife, come in then and call me gossip Quickly? coming in to borrow a mess of vinegar; telling me she had a good dish of prawns, whereby thou didst desire to eat some; whereby I told thee they were ill for a green wound? And didst thou not, when she was gone down stairs, desire me to be no more so familiarity with such poor people; saying that ere long they would call me Madam? And didst thou not kiss me and bid me fetch thee thirty shillings?

There, I think, we see Falstaff as he was, in a warm but not a flattering light; but with it we must take Mistress Quickly's last words to him when he goes off to the war:

> Well, fare thee well: I have known thee these twenty-nine years, comes peascod time; but an honester and truer-hearted man,—well, fare thee well.

In these few glimpses we see Falstaff in himself: an embodiment of universal humanity in one of its aspects, an immemorial figure confined to no age, over whose head changes of dynasties and civilisations might easily pass with no more effect than if they were stories read out of a book. But by a turn of events he is involved in history, caught and irrelevantly fixed at one pin-point of time, and becomes an anomalous sacrificial victim to the warring interests of the hour. This is what gives us the feeling of profound inconsistency. In our hearts we do not believe that he ever went to Shrewsbury; we feel that while the revolt flares up and is crushed, while Henry IV dies and the Prince steps on to the throne, Falstaff is still living his immemorial life in Eastcheap. We are never convinced that he was given a command, and empowered to recruit men. To make him do these things Shakespeare had to take him out of one world and set him down in another; and once there, he was left with no choice but to die of disappointment and a broken heart. Perhaps Shakespeare was tempted by the comic possibilities of showing him in a new setting; in any case the imagination protests at such a monstrous error. The fault is expiated in the wonderful account of Falstaff's death, in Mistress Quickly's words: 'The king has killed his heart', and in Bardolf's after his death: 'Would I were with him, wheresome'er he is, either in heaven or in hell'.

Panurge is not a character of such endless fascination

and interest as Falstaff; for though Rabelais is a very great writer, his greatness is of a different kind from Shakespeare's; it is predominantly philosophical and moral rather than imaginative. He has, of course, a powerful imagination, and an unsurpassed fancy, and a humorous gift beyond compare except with Shakespeare's; and Panurge is a great character, an immemorial embodiment of human nature like Falstaff himself, though not so great. He is essentially a man of sound natural appetites, and of great natural intelligence. As for the appetites, he is quite unashamed of them; as for the intelligence, he uses it freely to enquire into the plainest and subtlest problems that come within his reach. If it were not that he is naturally so sound and kind, we might easily see him becoming one of the typical Renaissance men whom we find in the Elizabethan drama, men like Edmund, or Flamineo, or Bosola, in whom appetite and intelligence are nakedly embodied, without any other quality to humanise them: a Macchiavellian. Panurge's combination of appetite and intelligence would have equipped him for such a part; but between him and that possibility stood the sanity of Rabelais' genius; for we feel that if Rabelais had been confronted with Macchiavelli, he would have roared with laughter. Consequently Panurge has always enough sound sense to know that appetite and intelligence goaded by ambition do not bring happiness or comfort of mind, but the opposite. His appetite therefore does not take the direction of acquisition, which is personal and selfish, but of enjoyment, which is general and gives at the same time what it takes; and his intelligence, though concentrated for such a long time on the question, Should he marry? And if so, would he become a cuckold? considers the subject from every point of view, till it becomes a discussion of universal scope. The appetite is sublimated in these larger considerations, without losing its natural quality; every personal question swells to an enormous size, and the vast dimensions of universal human nature presently appear. This accumulating power of the imagination, which is like the rolling of a great snowball, takes charge when Panurge and his friends begin talking; everything becomes gigantic, like the symbolical figures of the two benevolent giants themselves, Gargantua and Pantagruel. Panurge's plea for borrowing and lending leads by natural stages to a vision of the world in which there is neither, a vision almost as powerful as the evocation of universal chaos in *King Lear*:

> Venus will be no more Venerable, because she shall have lent nothing. The Moon will remain bloody and obscure: For to what end should the Sun impart unto her any of his Light? He owed her nothing. Nor yet will the Sun shine on the earth, nor the Stars send down any good Influence, because the Terrestrial Globe hath desisted from sending up their wonted Nourishment by Vapours and Exhalations. . . . Men will not then salute one another: it will be but lost labour to expect Aid or Succour from any, or to cry, Fire, Water, Murther, for none will put to their helping Hand. Why? He lent no money, there is nothing due to him. . . . In short, Faith, Hope and Charity would be quite banished from such a world; for Men are born to relieve and assist one another: and in their stead should succeed and be introduced Defiance, Disdain and Rancour, with the most execrable Troop of all Evils, all Imprecations and all Miseries. . . . And if conform to the pattern of this grievous, peevish and perverse World which lendeth nothing, you figure and liken the little World, which is Man, you will find in him a terrible justling Coyle and Clutter: The Head will not lend the sight of his Eyes to guide the Feet and Hands; the Legs will refuse to bear up the Body; the Hands will leave off working any more for the rest of the Members; the Heart will be weary of its continual Motion for the beating of the Pulse, and will no longer lend his Assistance; the Lungs will withdraw the use of their Bellows. . . . The Brains, in the interim, considering this unnatural course,

will fall into a raving Dotage, and withhold all feeling from the Sinews, and Motion from the Muscles: Briefly, in such a world without Order and Array, owing nothing, lending nothing, and borrowing nothing, you would see a more dangerous Conspiration than that which Aesope exposed in his Apologue. Such a World will perish undoubtedly; and not only perish, but perish very quickly.

One sees here how, starting from a fancy, Rabelais gets lost in a vision of universal anarchy. It is his insatiable mind that leads him on, his lust to embrace everything, and this enquiring awakens his imagination in turn, which is an intellectual imagination.

There remains the difference between the position Panurge and Falstaff occupy in their societies. Panurge is freely accepted by the Prince Pantagruel and his circle; Falstaff is cast out; his English surroundings cannot assimilate him. We can draw no very clear conclusions from this; for the simple reason that the world Rabelais describes is not France, but Utopia, and that his characters, unlike Shakespeare's, do not have to die. In portraying the relations between the kind Prince and Panurge, Rabelais is telling us what he thought was desirable and in certain circumstances possible. Panurge represents a natural potency of human nature which may be treated in two ways; it can be repressed or cast out to follow its own devices, or accepted and assimilated and civilised. In drawing Panurge into the majestic circle of Gargantua and Patangruel and making him in time an admirable though unconventional member of it, Rabelais acted symbolically in the tradition of what was once the French spirit, which conceived civilisation as an endlessly hospitable thing in which all the variety of human minds has a place.

EMMA BOVARY AND
BECKY SHARP

WE learn more about the similarities and differences between civilised countries from the figures in their imaginative literatures than from a critical study of their great writers. Panurge and Falstaff tell us more about English and French life than Shakespeare and Rabelais. They were created out of the heart of England and France, and the two great writers who portrayed them drew upon a source greater than themselves. The characters who fill the drama and fiction of a country are like a population, and embody its ordinary and extraordinary mode of life in a multitudinous image. The image is palpable to us, and there seems to be no means for dealing with it in literary criticism or literary history. Criticism is concerned with the truth and skill with which these characters are portrayed, and literary history is mainly confined to literary history. Yet without the figures in Rabelais and Molière and Balzac and Stendhal and Proust France would remain an abstraction for us. There should be some other way of using them.

This is an attempt to compare two famous imaginary figures and try to discover from them certain differences between the life of England and France. Emma Bovary and Becky Sharp do not obviously resemble each other, but they have one quality in common: they are both ambitious women. They should therefore tell us, among other things, something about ambition as it is felt in France and England, in private life, on a modest average, and what it is that colours in these two countries the ambition of the large class which wants to get from some social position to the one above it, since that is what ordinary ambition means.

First, the period in which these two women lived must be taken into account, since that determined the temporal shape of their characters. If Becky Sharp had been born a hundred years before she would have chosen other means to realise her aims. In *Esmond* Thackeray has drawn the portrait of such a woman. Beatrix Castlewood openly employs her physical charm to advance herself, while Becky does not. The reason is that Becky lived in an age when women were expected to show their sexual nature only in their bed-rooms, where the reader could not follow them. It was one of those periods of stupendous propriety which supervene when a new class emerges out of obscurity into power, and is afraid to do anything for fear of doing something unbecoming. Every thought and feeling had to be irreproachable, otherwise the world might not recognise that the newly arrived class had a valid right to arrive. It was the most unpromising society imaginable for an adventuress, so that instead of using her physical attraction Becky was forced to turn to her acquaintances something resembling the meek feminine mask they expected to see. This cost her a great effort and some renunciation. It made her an actress, and that is where she is most unlike Emma Bovary. The downfall of an actress is comedy, the defeat of a stratagem, not of a life; but Emma's downfall is tragedy, and she is completely in it. Yet, living in the Victorian Age, Becky had no choice but to be an actress; all the women in the uneasy middle class had to be whether they possessed the ability or not: it was an era of humble, well-meaning, bad actresses in their hundreds of thousands.

We have to think of the Industrial Revolution, and the new class it threw up, as the background to Becky Sharp. The world of Emma Bovary was still very little affected by that change. The manners of society had been coloured more by ideas than by material processes, as so often is the case in France, or so often seems to be. The catchwords of the French Revolution, conveniently diminished, had become the commonplaces on which bourgeois respectability supported itself. Also, the romantic movement had influenced the sentiments of the new middle class, as it had not done in England: there is no sign that Wordsworth, Coleridge and Shelley existed for the citizens of Vanity Fair. It is a vulgarised romanticism that leads to the death of Emma Bovary. She pursues a second-rate ideal of romantic love in a third-rate world. The civilisation in which Flaubert encloses, or rather traps her, is a complete though corrupt civilisation displayed in its various facets, social, political, moral, aesthetic; and her tragedy springs from dreams begotten by it which it cannot fulfil.

Becky lives in a far smaller and simpler world, a world of money values. Her ideal is a bank stuffed to the roof with money, and a merchant or lord stuffed to the eyes with good living. These are the means by which she hopes to establish herself in the very centre of respectability. She is resolved to reach a position; Emma tries to fulfil an ideal of life.

There is a moment when Emma and Becky seem to be very close to each other, for they say almost the same thing in different words. And that moment shows how far they are apart. After Emma's marriage to Charles Bovary, when she realises that he can never fulfil the dream she has been nursing, she cries:

'Pourquoi, mon Dieu! me suis-je mariée?'

184

The corresponding scene in *Vanity Fair* is the one where Sir Pitt Crawley unexpectedly proposes to Becky:

> Rebecca started back, a picture of consternation. In the course of this history we have never seen her lose her presence of mind; but she did now, and wept some of the most genuine tears that ever fell from her eyes.
>
> 'O Sir Pitt!' she cried, 'O sir—I—I'm married already.'

Becky is as disillusioned as Emma. But Emma suffers because a romantic ideal has miscarried, and Becky because she has missed a chance to marry a rich baronet by secretly marrying his indigent younger son.

To understand these two women one must next consider the great difference between the two men who created them. *Vanity Fair* and *Madame Bovary* both attempted something new. Flaubert planted himself outside society, as a judge. Thackeray discarded the conventional framework of fiction as it had been known, and pleased or shocked his readers by showing his characters moving about as they did in the actual world; something which was not done again, on a greater scale, until Tolstoy. He killed George Osborne by a chance bullet at Waterloo, just like Tolstoy. He knew he was doing something not done before, and that is the reason for the asides in which he wheedles or cajoles the reader. 'I know', he says towards the beginning of *Vanity Fair*

> that the tune I am piping is a very mild one (although there are some terrific chapters coming presently), and must beg the good-humoured reader to remember, that we are only discoursing at present about a stockbroker's family in Russell Square, who are taking walks, or luncheon, or dinner, or talking and making love as people do in common life, and without a single passionate and wonderful incident to mark the progress of their loves.

The terrific chapters do come, but they are terrific in a different style from Dickens. The book is filled with genius, and is the chief picture of Victorian life painted by a man of discriminating intelligence as well as of imagination. Thackeray saw the main lines of Victorian society, for he conformed to them and disliked them.

Flaubert's vision of society is as clear as Thackeray's, but it is more full and exact. Both men are alike in their critical view of society; they are unlike in every other way. Thackeray is a gregarious writer; Flaubert, a solitary writer. Thackeray speaks from the very middle of society; he is conscious of it in the same way that the eighteenth-century novelists were; that is to say, he is aware not only of the characters he is describing but of a circle of educated readers who are critically weighing his words, so that he falls naturally into a conversational tone. He appeals to a relatively small audience, for the circle of educated readers was narrowing; Flaubert appealed to no audience at all.

He stood aside from society and studied it objectively, as one might study the geological evidences of some past form of life. He did not stand apart in indifference, but because he wanted to see society as it was, without personal bias or attachment. He set down what he saw without any regard for what the reader might feel. Sometimes he gives the impression of a man speaking out of a solitude into a solitude; the author as a person and the reader as an object disappear: all that remains is the work itself. He has no grace but the grace of style, and that is exhibited for its own sake, because it is right, not because it is intended to please. He is the first representative of a new kind of literary artist, self-isolated for a specific purpose.

When the novelist stands aside from society and regards it simply as an object to be studied, something has gone wrong with society, or with the novelist, or with the relation between them. The novel is driven to live more and more on itself, instead of drawing upon the common fund of living. This implies in writers like Flaubert and Joyce a radical division in themselves between the human being and the novelist, a division which they deliberately cultivate. In being divided from society they are isolated from themselves. There seems to be no example among English novelists of this devotion and this isolation; Joyce was an Irishman and an exile.

The point is that Flaubert sees Emma Bovary from this position outside society and that Thackeray sees Becky Sharp from the middle of society. His judgment of Becky is accordingly a social judgment, while Flaubert's judgment of Emma is something less and something more; perhaps merely a judgment, intended to be of no obvious use: a sort of thing in itself. He makes us feel as no other novelist has done that something outside, neither the reader nor the writer, is judging the characters. This has a curious effect on them; we see Emma in isolation; we see Becky always among other people.

Thackeray and Flaubert had each a criticism of society, and its symbol was for Thackeray 'snobbery' and for Flaubert 'vulgarity'. The subject of their novels was the newly-risen middle class, and in it they saw two kinds of thought and feeling mingling, and mingling in such a way that they corrupted each other. For Thackeray snobbery did not stand for the sanctioned acceptance of superiority which belonged to the old ruling class, but for that which made the new class do anything to know or even be snubbed by a lord. For Flaubert vulgarity was something new, a sort of rash eating inward. He addressed a public afflicted by that disease. The new middle class now had the leading voice in society, but without possessing the intellectual capacity or the discrimination in human affairs, which entitled it to leadership. The result was a blunting of the finer apprehensions of the heart and the mind, a respectable fatuousness in the judgment of experience which one finds occasionally even in poets like Tennyson and Browning. The social position of the new middle class was false by choice; they had to assume a set of values and sentiments which did not in the least suit them, yet was the only decent covering they could find. As described by Thackeray, they did not use their wealth to acquire civilisation, but to push themselves into society or pretend that they belonged to it, and this corrupted the virtues which had brought them where they were. Behind all their activity one is aware of some principle of confusion, and behind that again there were the ideas of liberty, equality and fraternity in France, and in England their practical equivalents, the theories of *laissez-faire*, the struggle for life and the survival of the fittest: all of which denied society.

We have to look at Becky and Emma against this background where the old values were moribund and the new were vulgar and snobbish. Flaubert confessed that Emma was himself. Becky is not Thackeray in the same complete sense; yet she is like him in an important respect: that, while herself a snob, she sees through snobbery. The difference between them is that while Thackeray exposes snobbery, Rebecca uses it to advance her aims; she is what Thackeray might have been if he had not had a heart and a conscience. She is in the secret, like himself, and he has more respect for her than for old Osborne, the perfect believing snob, or his son George, though they are honest, and she is not honest at all. For she is honest to herself, though dishonest to every one else. She is the only character in the story who could understand what Thackeray is saying, and he treats her with the wry intimacy of one

who knows too much. Yet he was not able to draw her
completely; the conventions of the age and his own mixture of timidity and snobbery prevented him from dealing
with her with the frankness of a Fielding. He does occasionally hint that Becky may have given something in
exchange for the thousand pound note which Lord Steyne
left with her; he indicates that Steyne was a notorious
libertine; yet in the scene where her husband thrashes
him and goes to his friend Captain Macmurdo to arrange
a duel, Macmurdo says:

> 'She may be innocent after all. She says so. Steyne has been a
> hundred times alone with her in the house before.'

Later, when Becky, having failed with bigger game, drags
Jos Sedley round Europe at her heels, Thackeray again
hints at Becky's purity. Dobbin visits Joe secretly, hoping
to get him out of her claws:

> 'I swear to you—I swear it to you on the Bible', gasped out
> Joseph, wanting to kiss the book, 'that she is as innocent as a
> child, as spotless as your own wife.'

Thackeray shows Becky consorting with the worst inter-
national riff-raff, spongers and cheats and bullies. But
what she was doing in their company is only to be guessed
at; and half of her is left to our imaginations. The silence
about this side of her life gives her the appearance of
taking everything and giving nothing, and makes her
more repulsive than she would have been if Thackeray had
dealt frankly with her. She becomes an image of moral
corruption, without a heart.

Thackeray makes Becky all head, and her counterpart,
Amelia Sedley, all heart. Amelia changes in the course of
the story, but Becky does not; she is the same, and has the
same confidence in the head, at the end where she goes to
church, and is a devoted friend of the Destitute Orange

girl, the neglected Washerwoman, and the Distressed Mumnffian, as she was at the start when she disconcerted Miss Pinkerton of Chiswick Mall and set her cap at Joseph Sedley. Only her fortunes alter, for she is all head, and the head does not grow old, but only learns a few more tricks.

Being all head, one might have expected Becky to achieve social success. Instead she is a failure and has to console herself by assuming the title of Lady Crawley, and

> chiefly hangs about Bath and Cheltenham, where a very strong party of excellent people consider her to be a most injured woman. She has her enemies? Who has not? Her life is the answer to them. She busies herself in works of piety.

Yet she was a pretty young woman, with unusual intelligence and no scruples, and she was resolved to succeed. She failed through an over-confidence in her own quick mind, an excessive contempt for the stupidity of others, and a complete lack of the kind of understanding which comes only from the heart. She misconceived the human situation. The lack of a few ordinary impulses, against which she could not provide, since she was without them, was enough to spoil all her schemes. She stands outside society (like Flaubert, but for a very different reason), belongs to no class, and carries out a raid on society by means which society was not supposed to use. Her progress is a sort of pilgrim's progress conducting her to the semblance of respectability as a completely bogus yet not unrespected member of the aristocracy. One feels that we can read in her the great fable of the Victorian age.

Emma Bovary cannot be formulated like Becky. She does not know exactly what she wants, and can find for her longings only a vague dream filled with hackneyed romantic properties. In the beautiful chapter describing her life as a young girl in the convent school, Flaubert evokes her inner world with its lovers, its solitary pavilions, its dark forests, its knights brave as lions and gentle as lambs, always cap-a-pie, and weeping like fountains. Sultans, bayaderes, giaours, minarets, Roman ruins, nightingales, all the debris of romantic poetry are there, all second-hand, but taken together, as Flaubert manipulates them, composing an image of strange beauty. Her marriage to Charles and her response to it show the difference between her and Becky. We see Becky in action, and all of her goes into it. We see Emma more in reverie; we think of her gazing out through the window with her head supported on her hand; in action she fails, for nothing she does or feels can satisfy her imagination fed on the illusions of romantic poetry. Flaubert follows all her moods like a lover or an accuser; moods when the endless boredom of life in a small provincial town prostrates her, moods of repentance and recovery, of fortuitous happiness, of complete despair. He notes the variations in her health, the changes in her appearance. She grows thin, she looks taller, her eyes grow larger. She dresses with care, attends scrupulously to her housekeeping, and warms her husband's slippers against his return in the evening. She becomes slatternly, lies in bed most of the day, and neglects her child. The alternations of boredom lead to her first love affair with the vulgarian Rodolphe. He deserts her, she falls into deeper boredom and emerges in the arms of a second lover, a commonplace young man whom she idealises with more and more difficulty, maintaining her alliance with him by running up debts she cannot pay. The more persistently she pursues her dream of romantic love, the more it turns into a sort of forced sensuality. She is compelled to use all sorts of subterfuges, like Becky herself; but unlike Becky she is clumsy in her employment of them, for her passions are involved. Faced with ruin, she kills herself: a dreadful end such as neither Becky nor Thackeray would have contemplated.

What parallels and contrasts are we to draw from the study of these two women, and what light, if any, do they throw on the life of England and France? Both women are ambitious and dissatisfied, both cherish a dream of glory (if Becky's can be called a dream), and both fail to realise it. What strikes us first is that Becky's dream is practical and therefore limited; she might easily, with better luck, have married a baronet or even a peer. Though she tried to push her way among them, she did not regard the English upper classes romantically: what she admired in them was their solidity, power and comfort, which she wanted to acquire for herself. In this she was typical of the England in which she lived, the England of money values; but perhaps she was more generically English in her practical sense, which often ignores and sometimes despises the world of the mind and the imagination.

Emma Bovary's dream contained a great number of other things, difficult to define. She too longed for a life of comfort and privilege, but she thought of it qualitatively, in terms of elegance, and the cultivation of the imagination and the finer senses through a great love affair. If a French novelist had portrayed Becky Sharp he would not have entirely omitted such things as these. Even calculation as cool as hers would not have been divorced from passion, or the practical cut off so completely from the ideal. In Thackeray's Becky the separation is complete: the practical is one thing, the ideal another. Becky would no doubt have agreed that goodness and love were all very well in their own way; but money was real.

It was more real in the Victorian Age than it has ever been in England before or since. In the sixteenth century

the ideas of ambition and glory and love were closely associated. The change happened in the Industrial Revolution
when it was discovered that a man could get rich without
changing the quality of his life. Nevertheless one imagines
that this could not have happened at all but for the peculiar
illogical freedom of the English which permits them to
allot feeling and imagination and thought to one world,
and practice to another. It is an arrangement which makes
Becky Sharp possible on the one hand, and William Blake
on the other. It was implicitly accepted by the romantic
poets. When an English poet says that the world is too
much with us or speaks about passing beyond the farthest
bound of human thought, he speaks naturally, for he
speaks of the 'other world'. The English romantic poets
turned love into a pure spontaneous emotion which could
only become false if it were cultivated, and withered and
faded in a worldly atmosphere. There could be no connection between it and ambition, for it was not in 'the World'.
The only Victorian poet who saw love as a complex emotion, with its moods, its phases, its development, its relation to all sorts of things from business to art, was Browning, and he was neither typical nor popular. On the one
hand, among the many, a belief in practice so bigoted
that it distrusted or despised theory: on the other the imagination freely moving in a world of its own: that was
the English convention after the Industrial Revolution
and the Romantic Movement. It was not a satisfactory
one.

Compared with this loose, easygoing, dissociated freedom, French civilisation strikes one as incredibly concentrated, and confronts imagination with reality, practice
with theory, passion with thought, in a world where they
cannot get away from one another. This convention could
not accept the casual spirit of the English which leaves

people to pack into their lives what they can and let the rest go, leaving behind them that rich diversity of characters and oddities which we find in Dickens. Emma was trapped in the civilisation which moulded her: Becky is free to make her own choice.

JANE AUSTEN

WHEN you speak about a great writer that hundreds of others have written about, it is sometimes useful to approach the subject from an unexpected angle. There has been very little said about the sense of evil in Jane Austen's novels, and I propose to begin with that and see where it will lead me. Evil is not an overwhelming presence in her picture of life, of course, as it is, for instance, in Dostoevsky's. But it is there, as a necessary part of the picture, and there in proportion as everything is in her world. If it were not there, her picture would not be true; her sense of evil is part of her sense of proportion. The reason why so little attention has been paid to it may be that the scenes she describes are so circumscribed and ruled so strictly by polite convention, that we feel the characters cannot go very far in any direction, either for good or evil. Steventon, we feel, is not likely to harbour villains, so how could Miss Austen have met any. Nevertheless almost all her novels have a villain to show us, a weak villain in Mr. Wickham, for instance, a strong and unscrupulous villain in Mr. Walter Elliot, and in Henry Crawford, the most fascinating of them all, a man of great charm and intelligence, who seems to balance on the razor edge between good and evil, and is ruined finally by a quality which belongs both to virtue and vice, that is, amiability, in his case a too easy amiability. He wants to charm and to be liked; he wants that more than anything else in the world. At the same time he knows his weakness, without being able to overcome it; instead he nurses it and becomes more skilful in his use of it, and this at last corrupts his heart. When, almost in a panic, he tries to find safety in a marriage with Fanny Price, he finds he is too late. He has no doubt that poor Fanny will accept him; in thinking that, he also shows the flaw in his character. After she has rejected him he falls back on his old courses, yields to an extravagant impulse and runs away with Maria, a married woman whom he does not respect, ruining for nothing her life and his own. One feels that if he had married Fanny, he might have become good as well as intelligent and charming; and no doubt Fanny would have had a much more interesting life with him than she was to have with her dull, dear Edmund.

The interesting thing about Wickham and Henry Crawford is that they are genuinely attractive, especially to women; they have the attraction of the unknown and and the unpredictable. They are more immediately attractive than the husbands that Elizabeth Bennet and Fanny Price marry. Elizabeth, comparing Wickham with Darcy, finds her heart drawn towards the bad man and repelled by the good. She believes Wickham when he is telling her lies, and disbelieves Darcy when he is telling the truth. Evil is very attractive, Jane Austen seems to be telling us, but the attraction is a lie. It is judged by what comes of it, and in *Pride and Prejudice* that is the abduction of Lydia by Wickham and shame brought on the Bennet household. Lydia and Wickham, being below good and evil, are the only two who have no sense of the shame, except for foolish and fond Mrs. Bennet. As they will live after this by a sort of respectable blackmail on Darcy, they are ready to settle down to a life of shiftless folly. Lydia's father with his humorous enjoyment of his daughter's silliness, and her mother with her fond encouragement of it, are really responsible for the scandal; Mr. Bennet feels it as a scandal; Mrs. Bennet scarcely feels it at all. That indicates the difference in quality between them. Everything is set down in exact proportion, with an art that explains itself.

The distinction between good and evil in *Pride and Prejudice* is so clear that to point it out is almost superfluous. It is there as we read. But *Mansfield Park* is a more difficult book, indeed the only novel of Jane Austen's that leaves us sometimes at a loss. Lionel Trilling, an intelligent critic, says some things about it which are suggestive and true, and some which seem to me to be quite off the mark. He takes Jane Austen seriously, and as she is a great writer she should be taken seriously. But he surely takes her with the wrong kind of seriousness when he enlists Hegel to explain her. He begins by saying: 'Sooner or later, when we speak of Jane Austen, we speak of her irony, and it is better to speak of it sooner rather than later because nothing can so far mislead us about her work as the wrong understanding of this one aspect of it'. After this he defines what irony means in its various uses, and concludes that 'What we may call Jane Austen's first or basic irony is the recognition of the fact that spirit is not free, that it is conditioned, that it is limited by circumstance. This, as everyone knows from childhood on, is indeed an anomaly. Her next and consequent irony has reference to the fact that only by reason of this anomaly does spirit have virtue and meaning.' There is something true hidden in these large generalisations; but it is a mistake in a critic to employ a language which would have appeared quite strange to the writer he is dealing with. Mr. Trilling is not in Jane Austen's world at all, it seems to me, when he makes his observations on irony and spirit; he is in his own world, a great distance away. And when, employing this dialectic, he comes to the conclusion that

Mansfield Park confuses and repels so many readers because in it Jane Austen turned her irony against itself, and was ironical about irony, I feel I cannot measure the distance between these two minds working in quite different ways. Jane Austen, I feel quite sure, would not have used a word like spirit, nor would she have been perturbed by recognising the fact that spirit is conditioned and not free; she knew too well that human beings are limited, which means the same thing; she had a sense of proportion.

I do not believe myself that the central virtue of Jane Austen lies in her irony; I think her chief virtue is finer and that it is the virtue of proportion. In her sense of proportion she is almost perfect; yet in *Mansfield Park* it now and then deserts her. In spite of this it is a great novel, as Mr. Trilling claims. But he holds that its greatness is 'commensurate with its power to offend', and there again I cannot agree with him. He reports that the many students with whom he has read Jane Austen found in the other novels 'a great deal to say to them about the modern personality', but that *Mansfield Park* was the exception, and was bitterly resented. Mr. Trilling explains this by saying: 'It scandalises the modern assumptions about social relations, about virtue, about religion, sex, and art. Most troubling of all is its preference for rest over motion. To deal with the world by condemning it, by withdrawing from it and shutting it out, by making oneself and one's modes and principles of life the very centre of existence and to live the round of one's days in the stasis and peace thus contrived—this, in an earlier age, was one of the recognized strategies of life, but to us it seems not merely impractical but almost wicked.'

After this I feel I have a long road to go to get back to *Mansfield Park*. It is a great novel, but it has faults that are not present in the others. Perhaps one of the reasons for this is given in a letter quoted by Mr. Trilling. Writing to her sister Cassandra, Jane says that the subject of the novel was to be 'ordination'. Her father and two of her brothers were clergymen and the subject was to her hand. Another reason may have been that she found *Pride and Prejudice*, as she says in another letter to Cassandra, 'rather too light, and bright, and sparkling'. And perhaps still another is that she took as her heroine a feminine type already too much written about before her time. In the novels of Susan Ferrier, a Scottish writer, and of Elizabeth Wetherell in America, there always appears a gentle, obedient, passive young woman who in spite of the persecution of her parents and guardians always manages to evade the man whom they want her to marry, and to marry the man of her choice. The type goes back to Richardson, to *Pamela* with its happy ending, and to *Clarissa* with its tragedy. Perhaps tragedy should be the true ending to stories of this kind, for only it can add dignity to such patience and constancy; but when these qualities are found to work, when they do not have to pass any final test but instead pay a sound profit, we feel we are being put off by something bogus, and that our sympathies have been exploited. I fancy that Jane Austen may have found as she went on that Fanny Price was inevitably becoming a stock character, a moral cliché, and that there was little she could do with her, or with the clergyman whom she had set her heart on marrying. The faults in *Mansfield Park* are genuine faults, and not due to Jane's decision to be ironical about irony. Yet it contains some of the most extraordinary scenes that she ever imagined. She could at any time draw a passive and gentle character. Jane Bennet is patient and uncomplaining, and Anne Elliot still more patient and uncomplaining, and she is the most exquisite portrait of a woman that

Jane Austen ever drew, and the one she loved most herself, as one can tell by the tenderness of the portrayal. No; Fanny Price is unconvincing because Jane found her conforming to a whole line of stock characters. Fanny could not help turning into the meek young girl who had got her own way in story after story.

What makes *Mansfield Park* so fascinating is that in it Jane Austen attempts something which she was not to attempt again on the same scale. It was written after the success of *Pride and Prejudice*. She was not satisfied with that novel, and was eager to show that she could write something different. After Elizabeth Bennet, who was all wit and energy, she would draw a heroine all submission and pathos. After describing a social scene, she would deal with the serious theme of ordination. She did not succeed in either of these aims. Edmund, dedicated to the church, is the dullest, deadest character she ever drew. But the seriousness of her aim produced its effect nevertheless. Compared with *Pride and Prejudice*, *Mansfield Park* is like a full-scale study of corruption. The Crawfords, Mary and Henry, are at the heart of it; the corruption spreads from them. They are witty, delightful, intelligent, seductive, and they come from London; Mr. Trilling points out that sophisticated and delicate corruption is generally believed to belong to the metropolis. The intimacy between brother and sister, the way in which they speak to each other when they are alone, without any pretence that they acknowledge any moral standard, shows what they are. At the same time, though they hardly admit it to themselves, they have generous impulses and, given the chance, they are both capable of living a better life. They even desire it at odd moments, without confessing it to each other. These two extraordinary creatures are welcomed into a house where the father, Sir Thomas Bertram, a strict formal man,

is away on business, and where the mother is a lazy, help-
less, selfish woman. They make friends with the two
daughters, Maria and Julia, who are avid for pleasure and
excitement, which the Crawfords can easily supply. Henry
flirts with both daughters in turn, and rouses a jealousy
between them which he enjoys. Maria is engaged to a dull
but rich young man, with a splendid estate, and she turns
to Henry for distraction. Julia, who is free, thinks she
should have Crawford for herself, and is furiously jealous
of Maria. Mary Crawford, in spite of herself, half falls in
love with Edmund, the younger son of the house who
intends to enter the church; but she does all she can to
make his career ridiculous to him. All these complicated
passions and jealousies are concentrated within the walls of
Mansfield Park. And finally, all is seen through the meek,
watchful and prudish eyes of Fanny Price, the only Victorian character that Jane Austen ever drew.

This collection of people, at odds with each other, and
ready for mischief, decide to act a play, and choose a
somewhat ambiguous one. The excitement of the rehearsals
inflame their passions, and impersonation, as Mr. Trilling
points out, is itself a real forbidden passion. A situation
which might have resolved itself harmlessly assumes all
the marks of danger. The fuss made in the book about the
amateur theatricals has often been dismissed as ridiculous.
But the whole situation has to be taken into account. The
damage done in the play leads finally to Maria's running
away with Henry Crawford from her husband, and the
ruin of two lives. An additional shade of guilt is cast upon
the affair by the fact that Sir Thomas Bertram is at sea and
in possible danger, and the knowledge that he would dis-
approve of what they were doing. Jane Austen herself had
no dislike of private theatricals; we know that her family
were very fond of them. It is the situation that justifies her

treatment of this scene, and that gives it a masterly touch of the forbidden and the corrupt.

In *Mansfield Park* there are other episodes as fine and as subtle as this. Maria Bertram is engaged to Rushworth, who is stupid and rich and whom she does not love. The Bertrams and the Crawfords and Fanny Price pay a visit to Sotherton, Rushworth's estate. There the two sisters try to pair off with Henry Crawford. Maria wins, but she is encumbered with the presence of her intended husband. Fanny, as usual, is left quite alone, for Edmund has wandered away with Mary Crawford. Crawford and Rushworth have been talking of improvements to the gardens and the estate. They and Maria sit down on a seat near Fanny, and go on discussing the possibility of improvements with great animation.

Maria Bertram and Crawford long to walk into the park in front of them, towards a knoll where they could have 'the requisite command of the house'. But the gate leading into it is locked, and Mr. Rushworth has not the key with him. After some polite bullying he declares that he will fetch it and goes off, Crawford takes his opportunity to rally Maria.

'You have a very smiling scene before you.'

'Do you mean literally or figuratively? . . . But unluckily that iron gate, that ha-ha, give me a feeling of restraint and hardship. I cannot get out, as the starling said.' As she spoke, and it was with expression, she walked to the gate; he followed her. 'Mr. Rushworth is so long fetching this key!'

'And for the world you would not get out without the key and without Mr. Rushworth's authority and protection, or I think you might with little difficulty pass round the edge of the gate here, with my assistance. I think it might be done, if you really wished to be more at large, and could allow yourself to think it not prohibited.'

How much there is in that passage, and how clearly it reveals what the characters feel by describing what they say, or say in riddles. When Maria cries, 'I cannot get out', does she know that it is the marriage she means and not the gate? One might suspect Jane Austen of a sort of symbolism, and I know that it is the custom just now to discover symbolism in the work of any writer. Jane Austen was no symbolist, but she certainly knew what she was doing when she wrote this passage; she was conveying with the utmost lucidity a situation which could not have been as well conveyed by the most exhaustive analysis. But Maria's word-play with the gate is something, I think, quite unique in Jane Austen's novels, and something which strikes one as being distinctively modern.

The exquisite moral discrimination of Jane Austen has never been questioned except by those, like Mark Twain and Charlotte Brontë, who find nothing to praise in her work. The discrimination is steady and unflinching. But her central image of evil is embodied in a succession of questionable young men, who stand like heraldic signs in her picture of life. Willoughby and Frank Churchill, careless and amiable and yet bringing disaster or the threat of it; Henry Crawford, playing with danger and inflicting social ruin on himself and a woman he does not love; Wickham, a commonplace, external, obvious rascal; and Walter Elliot, the bad man no longer young, the only obviously disagreeable bad man in the novels, the last image Jane Austen was to create of this figure who haunted her. Elliot is like a Wickham polished and made by art. These young men are her embodiment of temptation. Women are not the tempters to her, but these ambiguous attractive figures who cannot be trusted. They should have grown up, but they have not, and so they have the charm and the irresponsibility of youth. When her heroines marry, they choose men of maturity, who are more eminent for good-sense than for charm.

Was her judgment here as certain as it was in most other things? One hardly dares to ask the question. But in her last book, that exquisite masterpiece *Persuasion*, she seems to be asking the question herself. Anne Elliot once agreed to follow the advice of her friend Lady Russell, and rejected the man she loved because his prospects were uncertain. She remained in love with him afterwards. When she meets him again, after several years, in Bath, his position is established; he is Captain Wentworth, an eligible, successful officer in the Navy. For a time, though they meet, they are divided by misunderstanding, and by the attentions of Walter Elliot to Anne, which Wentworth misunderstands. Finally they come together. But now the qualities which Jane Austen attributes to her good and bad men appear to have interchanged. The good have the qualities of the bad, and the bad of the good. Elliot is outwardly distinguished by good-sense like Darcy and Knightley, and Wentworth by candour and charm like Frank Churchill. Elliot is, apart from all this, a thoroughly bad man, and Wentworth a good man. Yet Anne still does not know this when she reflects upon them: 'Mr. Elliot', she told herself, 'was rational, discreet, polished; but he was not open. There was never any burst of feeling, any warmth of indignation or delight, at the evil or good of others.' This, to Anne, was a decided imperfection. Her early impressions were incurable. She prized the frank, the open-hearted, the eager character beyond all others. Warmth and enthusiasm did captivate her still. She felt that she could so much more depend upon the sincerity of those who sometimes looked or said a careless or a hasty thing than of those whose presence of mind never varied, whose tongue never slipped.

While she makes this comparison between Elliot and Wentworth she is still thinking sensibly as Elizabeth

Bennet did, yet thinking differently. The balance between sense and sensibility has changed for her and for Jane Austen too; the wisdom of the heart has replaced the confidence of the head. There is still a balance, but it is a different balance. And that is the reason why there is a poetry and a tenderness in *Persuasion* which is lacking in the other novels. The difference is shown most clearly in the passage where Anne and Wentworth discover that they have always loved each other.

Jane Austen died at the age of forty-one. *Persuasion* is a promise of what she might have done, if she had lived. As it is, she remains the most perfect artist who ever attempted the English novel.

THE DARK FELICITIES OF
CHARLES DICKENS

THE astonishing development of Dickens' imagination in the last great novels is shown in two things: most obviously in his use of the plot, but also in a noticeable change of style. To take the plot first: in the early stories a comfortable hiatus yawns between it and the characters. Then, beginning tentatively with *Dombey and Son*, there is a change. The characters no longer appear and disappear to appear again when they are wanted: instead there is a large coherent design in which all the figures have their place, and the action moves towards a pre-ordained end. The order is so strictly maintained, the complication so carefully worked out, that the effect is almost oppressive. The early stories breathe a freedom in which we do not believe: in *Bleak House* and *Little Dorrit* all has become necessity. But the sense of oppression in these novels has a further cause, for in them Dickens at last finds his theme, and theme and plot are one: without the plot it would have been impossible to state the theme. The careless improvisation of the early stories is gone.

In these the plot runs on, carrying the characters on its back wherever Dickens chooses to take them. Or to change the picture, the story is like an enormous miscellaneous lodging-house or casual ward crammed with a fantastic variety of figures. The inmates come and go, grow rich or poor, become happy or unfortunate, but not generally as a consequence of their actions. The plot follows them about like a tireless messenger and looks after them like a busy housemaid.

These figures belong to two classes, and are either conventional heroes and heroines and villains, or caricatures. These two tribes come together in the story, yet live in different worlds, and not so much in time as in some place next door to it. Dickens treats them as if they were in the same world. Young Martin Chuzzlewit gets into trouble through his pride and selfishness, but reforms in time to share in the happy ending. This confronts Dickens with a dilemma; for if Martin is rewarded, obviously Pecksniff, although he is a mere caricature, an incarnation of hypocrisy, must be punished; and how can one punish a personification? The mixed plot brings up this difficulty again and again, where character and caricature have no choice but to falsify each other. This comes out most clearly in the final distribution of approval and blame.

A character in a novel, or in real life, is a man more than usually himself. A caricature, or a humour, is a figure unchangeably himself. He is totally there at every moment, so that we cannot think of him as having developed into what he is, or as developing into what he will be. He has no past and no future, but only an unchanging present. Sairey Gamp was never young, and Sam Weller will never grow old. They cannot be forced through time but only conducted through space, from scene to scene, not from year to year. Yet the conventional characters, thin as they are in the early stories, exist in time; weeks and years matter to them, if only because time must move in order to bring the happy ending. The caricatures, perfectly comfortable where they are, become unreal when they are thrust out into time and change into human beings; and when at the end of *David Copperfield* Micawber is sent to Australia to become a successful man, he might as well have been sent to the moon. We accept such things, infatuated by the brilliance of Dickens' gifts, yet we know that these last chapter arrangements are absurd. In the later novels we have no need to make such allowances.

The humours in the early stories are wonderful creations; they live after all on the outskirts of Falstaff's world. But there came a point in Dickens' development when they could not serve him any longer. He still reproduces them mechanically now and then in *Bleak House* and *Little Dorrit*, his two greatest novels, but they have lost their reality and are like caricatures of a caricature, or simple characters excessively overdrawn. Harold Skimpole is not a figure of flesh and blood like Sam Weller, but a trick which has grown facile, of which Dickens has grown weary.

What is it that we see happening in the late great novels? Something which can almost be called a change of heart; the desire for a deeper scrutiny of life where, after so much false pity, true pity can have a place. Dickens reached this new seriousness by taking as his central subject a theme which had appeared fitfully and erratically in his novels. It was the theme of imprisonment in its various forms, in actual prison, but also outside. The novels show the gradual, reluctant development of that theme. As everyone knows, Dickens' father had been more than once in prison for debt, and he himself as a boy had spent those wretched weeks in the blacking factory, where he felt that everyone had forsaken him. He never forgot these things, and they roused his anger to the end of his life. So again and again in the early stories there is a prison scene. Mr. Pickwick has to spend a short time in the Marshalsea through no fault of his own, and Micawber must live in fear of imprisonment while he goes about his precarious callings. We know that Pickwick will come out again; we know that Micawber will go in again. Accordingly prison is becoming more serious to him, being both behind Micawber and still to come. There is one short scene in *David Copperfield* where the prison suddenly undergoes an abominable change; the scene where David and Traddles find Micawber shedding sentimental tears as he gazes at the outer walls of the Marshalsea, within which he once felt safe from the ordinary dangers of freedom; we see his whole life then in a flash, but never again. Dickens is still playing hide and seek with imprisonment. For though Micawber is drawn from John Dickens, he is not David's father in the book, and David is not involved with him except as an acquaintance, so that he can escape, by a shift common in the early stories, to comfort and ease. He is not committed, nor is Dickens as yet.

It is doubtful whether without the example and encouragement of Wilkie Collins Dickens could have written his two masterpieces. Collins had shown how the elaborate technique of the mystery story, where light was brought from many sides on an inexplicable happening, could be used to give a picture of a section of Victorian society. He employed it for a relatively trivial purpose. Dickens seized upon it and made it a means for understanding the life of his time. He started from a central point, the Court of Chancery in *Bleak House*, and the Circumlocution Office in *Little Dorrit*, and from there the true nature of these horrible institutions was revealed in their immediate or remote effects on the lives of characters drawn from every class. The light cast outwards from these symbols of evil was in turn cast back upon them again.

The symbols used by Dickens in these two novels may appear inadequate, but only if we regard them apart from the way in which they are employed. Extracted from any work of imagination, all symbols seem poor and obvious;

it is the embodiment that gives them life. All that is required is that there should be a starting point capable of becoming the central point. Dickens reached that stage in his two greatest novels and achieved his first coherent and tragic picture of society.

In the early stories he is concerned mainly with some urgent topic, some social wrong of the time; and the comic relief is given by the humours, who live anyhow and anywhere. These stories illustrate the injustices of society for a moral purpose, and the moral purpose dictates the plot. The social criticism is expressed in a tone of confident indignation. What Dickens achieves in *Bleak House* and *Little Dorrit* is the *embodiment* of society in a vast collection of characters fatally or lightly touched by the power at the heart of it, which frustrates them all. *Bleak House* does not deal with actual imprisonment; yet the characters are seen as prisoners—of delay and hardhearted muddle—and we feel that Victorian society is the prison. In *Little Dorrit*, as Mr. Edmund Wilson has pointed out, we are presented with a whole collection of prisons: Mrs. Clennam is imprisoned for life in her Biblical Puritanism and her guilty secret, Casby the slum landlord in his greed and hypocrisy, his tenants in their poverty, the false Victorian millionaire in his secret terrors; and the people they meet (and sometimes people they never meet) are helplessly involved, through friendship, or calculation, or snobbery, or mere misfortune. Because of the complacent stupidity of the Circumlocution Office William Dorrit degenerates for twenty-five years in prison. The only one who escapes the contamination is his daughter Little Dorrit, born in prison, who is saved by self-abnegation; she does not respond, and even in prison is free.

Little Dorrit sets a theoretical problem; what would happen to a man as volatile as John Dickens and as irresponsible as Micawber if he had to spend twenty-five years in prison, and were afterwards to find himself rich and free and thrown into the whirl of society? It was a case quite outside Dickens' experience; John Dickens had been in prison, but never for long. Imagination was a faculty which he had employed hitherto in brilliant flashes; now it had to trace the gradual and prolonged degeneration of the man whom Micawber might have been had he not been safely swaddled in the caricature. To achieve this Dickens required a new form, where life and circumstance, character and fate were made to act upon one another: a plot which could become the living image of his conception. Nothing in Dickens is more wonderfully imagined than the slow degeneration of William Dorrit under imprisonment and during his last few years of freedom. To compare Dorrit with Micawber is to see the great change in the years between.

The change required not only a new kind of plot, but also a new style, capable of intimate revelation. In the two great novels it comes and goes, alternating between the confident condemnation of the earlier style and that curious exactitude which the deeper study of life brought him. He writes in the one style about the Circumlocution Office, and in the other about William Dorrit in prison, alternating between confident condemnation, where he is sure of the reader's support, and minute observation of suffering, with flashes of wonderful felicity. Nothing he had written before very much resembles the description in *Bleak House* of the neglected properties of the Court of Chancery:

> It is a street of perishing blind houses, with their eyes stoned out; without a pane of glass, without so much as a window frame, with the bare shutters tumbling from their hinges and falling asunder; the iron rails peeling away in flakes of rust; the chimneys sinking in; the stone steps to every door (and every door

might be Death's door) turning stagnant green; the very crutches on which the ruins are propped, decaying.

There the houses suffer with human suffering, are one with their tenants, and silently accuse the Court of Chancery. In a sentence Dickens suggests the subtle degradation of respectable servants of Chancery:

> Mr. Vholes put his dead glove, which scarcely seemed to have any hand in it, on my fingers, and then on my guardian's fingers, and took his long thin shadow away.

These felicities are scattered through *Bleak House*, and more thickly through *Little Dorrit*. There is, for instance, the wonderful account of the motley crowd who tended the shady needs of the prisoners in Marshalsea, degraded themselves and degraded by their work and the place:

> All of them wore the cast-off clothes of other men and women; were made up of patches and pieces of other people's individuality, and had no sartorial existence of their own proper. Their walk was the walk of a race apart. They had a peculiar way of doggedly slinking round the corner, as if they were eternally going to the pawnbroker's. When they coughed, they coughed like people accustomed to be forgotten on door-steps and in draughty passages, waiting for answers to letters in faded ink, which gave the recipients of those manuscripts great mental disturbance and no satisfaction. As they eyed the stranger in passing, they eyed him with borrowing eyes—hungry, sharp, speculative as to his softness if they were accredited to him, and the likelihood of his standing something handsome. Mendacity on commission stooped in their high shoulders, shambled in their unsteady legs, buttoned and pinned and darned and dragged their clothes, frayed their button-holes, leaked out of their figures in dirty little ends of tape, and issued from their mouths in alcoholic breathings.

In *Little Dorrit* one is struck by the close association between house and tenant, the human being and the rags he wears. Clennam, after being abroad for a long time, visits the house of the slum landlord Casby, with whose daughter he had once been in love. The house itself tells us what Casby is by picturing the secrecy in which he lives behind his mask.

> Clennam stepped into the sober, silent, air-tight house—one might have fancied it to have been stifled by Mutes in the Eastern manner— and the door, closing again, seemed to shut out sound and motion. The furniture was formal, grave, and quaker-like, but well-kept; and had as prepossessing an aspect as anything, from a human creature to a wooden stool, that is meant for much use and is preserved for little, can ever wear. There was a grave clock, ticking somewhere up the staircase; and there was a songless bird in the same direction, pecking at his cage, as if he were ticking too. The parlour fire ticked in the grate. There was only one person on the parlour-hearth, and the loud watch in his pocket ticked audibly.

It is a picture of mild and safe damnation, sanctioned and approved by the Circumlocution Office; the imprisoned bird and the clocks and watches calmly ticking it away. These images of houses and lives decaying through sanctified neglect and public selfishness, of ends of tape leaking from borrowed clothes, are like nothing in the early Dickens, and evoke with an exactitude which is a kind of felicity his new vision of the society in which he lived. The felicities in the book are dark felicities, and wound and delight us at the same time; there is hardly one which does not do both.

When we turn to these dark masterpieces from the earlier novels, we have the feeling that Dickens, by a deepening of his imaginative understanding, has at last accepted society, if acceptance is that final act which enables us to see things clearly. This does not prevent him from arraigning the Court of Chancery and the Circumlocution Office in his early indignant style; but the style is too light, and is thrown back from these impassive keeps without making any impression on them. They had enraged him once; now he understood them. We feel they are immovable, or incapable of movement, and so they transcend the generations, and are like spectral emanations produced by the mere fact of human living. They, or some temporal incarnation of them, will always be there, and so it is not society but human nature that is being arraigned. Dickens turns to these institutions in anger and cries: See what you have done with human lives. But the dark powers are more tenacious than the human lives, and a shadowy Court of Chancery, under another name, will still grind on. The earlier novels had helped to bring about reforms; but there is no reforming these shadowy institutions, which wait like poor demented Miss Flit for a decision 'on the Day of Judgement'. They bring degradation into the lives of countless people, and *Bleak House* and *Little Dorrit* describe on a sweeping scale that universal process, to be escaped from only by a man or a woman here and there, through unusual courage or abnegation or grace. This is the picture these two books leave on the mind. The institutions and the degradation alike are produced by human life in its weakness, ignorance, cupidity and folly. Dickens pities the weakness and the ignorance and the cupidity and the folly, and the misfortunes they bring, yet he continues his fight against the power, whatever it is, that brings them about. Indeed the fight is more intense, and is given a new sharpness by understanding. Faced with that power, he does not renounce hope. Perhaps that is what acceptance means.

THE POETIC IMAGINATION

BEFORE considering the use of the poetic imagination and what I mean by it, I should mention one
simple respect in which it is distinguished from
the scientific imagination. The poetic imagination cannot
prove or demonstrate, but only divine and persuade. We
know that scientists have sometimes divined truths long
before they could be proved; but the real achievement of
science lies in the proof. The poetic imagination can never
reach that point, nor has it any wish to do so; it remains in
its own world of inspired or uninspired guess-work; what
it says may be either true or false, and there is no means,
as there is in science, for demonstrating that it is the one
or the other. There is only what we call judgment. Science
advances from what is known to what is possible to be
known; and everyone is aware now, no matter how vaguely,
how great its advance has been in the last hundred years.
People know this not through any acquaintance with pure
science, but by the use of their eyes and other senses, and
the alteration which has come over the world around them.
Compared with this, the poetic imagination shows no
advance at all, and still does what it did in the time of
Homer. Literary conventions change, it is true; literary
movements appear and having exhausted themselves are
left behind by other movements. The Elizabethan age was
followed by an age of religious meditation, then by an age
of reason, then by the Romantic revival, and lastly by the
movement in this century whose chief representative is
Mr. Eliot. Looking at these movements, we see that they

215

do not complete or fulfil the movements which preceded them, but seem to arise rather out of dissatisfaction with them, a sense that one way of looking at life has grown too narrow or been too blindly accepted. In other words, there is something else to say, and in imaginative literature, so far as one can foresee, there will always be something else to say, for no image of life can ever be sufficient and final. There are, of course, in poetry and the story, things which are final, otherwise they would not be understood by later generations, or even by their own; yet the circumstances of life change, slowly or rapidly, and every age expects from the imagination a new effort and the creation of a contemporary image. Nevertheless these images, in their succession, do not obliterate or supersede or make obsolete those that came before them, and this is where poetic imagination differs so greatly from that of science. Old scientific treatises are read, I imagine, out of curiosity or as part of the history of science. But we do not read Homer or the stories in the Old Testament out of literary curiosity or an interest in the history of literature. We read Homer as we read Tolstoy, or to come nearer, as we read Henry James. The historian can of course help us to understand more completely the ideas and actions of the characters in the *Iliad*; yet without the aid of history we recognise these figures immediately as we read, and are again moved by their fate as if time did not matter. It is true, again, that different ages have passed different judgments on great writers. The eighteenth century did not see Shakespeare as his contemporaries did, nor as Coleridge did later, nor as we do now; yet it saw a real Shakespeare of its own. Then there are writers who sink into the background for a long time and suddenly reappear as cardinal influences on literature; I think of John Donne and his rediscovery by Sir Herbert Grierson. But these are tricks of time; for though it is true that every work of imagination is born in and is true for its time, what is important is that it remains true for other times, or in the old rhetorical phrase, for all time. And if that is so, the great figures in imaginative literature are perpetually contemporary, as I think Mr. Eliot has said; and that is what we feel them to be as we read about them. They never become history. Ancient or modern, they live in the perpetual present of mankind, crowding it with an accumulation of life and a living variety of human experience.

Regarding rationally the multitude of figures and passions presented by the imagination, we may find it strange that, instead of being content with our own troubles, we should be moved, sometimes so intensely, by the troubles of men and women long dead. Shakespeare, who retold the tragedies of Troilus and of Anthony, seems to have been struck with wonder at this when he makes Hamlet exclaim, after listening to the poor player bursting his heart over the sorrows of the mobled Queen:

What's Hecuba to him, or he to Hecuba?

And in a dialogue of Plato, 'Ion; or of the Iliad', Socrates was teased by the same mystery, and concluded that the poet does not achieve his effects by any rule of art but by inspiration, in a state of madness, and as if possessed by a spirit not his own; but that while any vestige of reason remains in him he is totally incapable of producing poetry. Yet the madness is a divine madness, and Socrates acknowledged that the poet is a thing ethereally light, winged and sacred.

The value of this dialogue lies in the way in which it shows that seen through the eyes of pure intelligence poetry is irrational by its nature and irrational in its effects; a truth which daily acquaintance with poetry often makes us forget. So that there is some justification in Socrates' conclusion and some excuse in what may seem the excessively romantic terms in which he states it. One of the reasons for this is that he was thinking of spoken poetry and of an audience moved immediately by it, whose presence helped to generate and intensify the divine madness. Now that we read poetry in books or listen to it being read by a disembodied voice on the Third Programme, it is difficult for us to believe that the poet is divinely mad. The solitary reader is more critical than the tens of thousands who assembled to hear Ion reciting Homer; he is not so easily moved, or moved not in the same way; the only modern parallel to Ion's performances is in the theatre, where people still sometimes shed tears and look earnestly at the actors in a tragedy. Coleridge's famous definition gives a more convincing idea of the imagination when it becomes productive:

> a more than usual state of emotion with more than usual order; judgment ever awake and steady self-possession with enthusiasm and feeling profound or vehement.

I think Middleton Murry implicitly adopted the theory of being carried away when he said that Shakespeare *was* Hamlet and Macbeth and Othello. That is no doubt true in a sense; but Shakespeare himself was there too, a watchful spectator and conductor of the spectacle. Novelists tell us again that their characters have sometimes completely surprised them; yet the fact that they were surprised shows that they had something of the ever-awake judgment of which Coleridge speaks. We must think of the imaginative writer as being both inside and outside the figures and emotions he describes. Wordsworth writes of certain states in which we see into the life of things, and it is the seeing that matters; without that there would be nothing but an intense inarticulate feeling.

Rilke gives a vivid account of this experience. He was fond of the 'einsehen', to insee, a state to which he became more and more addicted in his later poetry. In a letter he gives a vivid but one-sided idea of the mingled absorption and detachment of the imagination in dealing with the objects of its attention. The example he chooses is, I think, deliberately intended to be prosaic.

> I love inseeing. Can you imagine with me how glorious it is to insee, for example, a dog as one passes by—insee (I don't mean in-spect, which is only a kind of human gymnastic, by means of which one immediately comes out again on the other side of the dog, regarding it merely, so to speak, as a window upon the humanity lying behind it; no, not that)—but to let oneself precisely into the dog's very centre, the point from which it begins to be a dog, the place in it where God, as it were, would have sat down for a moment when the dog was finished in order to watch it under the influence of its first embarrassments and inspirations and to nod that it was good, that nothing was lacking, that it could not have been better made. For a while one can stand being right inside the dog, but one must be careful to jump out in time, before its environment has quite enclosed one, since otherwise one would simply remain in the dog and be lost for everything else.

That tells us a great deal about Rilke and something about the operation of the poetic imagination, though I feel that there is a chronological inaccuracy in the account of it. The absorption comes first and the detachment after, while they should, according to Coleridge, be simultaneous. Rilke was an unusually susceptible poet; he makes us feel that he could not resist the dog and then that he could not endure being confined in it and must save himself by jumping out again; he had a very strong sense of self-preservation. His curious life and his skill in jumping out of love affairs when they showed signs of committing him are proof enough of that. Yet by his 'inseeing' he could let himself into the centre of things, beasts, plants, fruits, affections and passions; though at the same time he shrank from human affection. This is what gives his poetry, fine as it is, its peculiar quality, a tumultuous movement and simultaneously a strange lack of tension. His curious theory of poetry follows, it may be, from this: his idea that the task of the poet is to make the visible invisible, and possess and discard the whole visible world, invisibly, within himself. I cannot enter into that excessive claim, but it throws some light on the case of the dog. If you let yourself into the centre of the dog, you may understand it but you will no longer see it; neither you nor the dog will be there. The normal working of the imagination is different; it both enters into and sees, is both inside and outside. Its dog is a different dog, a creature of a thousand moods observable by the eye and in movement, a young dog, an old dog, a playful dog, a surly dog. Actually Rilke's dog is little more than a Platonic idea.

For the imagination, as it is employed by the poet, the story-teller, the dramatist and the novelist, is the faculty by which life is grasped in its individual forms, and human beings and all living things are shown as they live and move. It cannot and does not wish to arrest its imagined figures so as to submit them to a precise examination, for it is in their movement that they live. At most it can convince us that they are real and induce a mood of belief. Sometimes these figures when we meet them in a novel may strike us with a sense of their familiarity, as if we had met them before and known them in real life. On the other hand they may appear quite strange to us, so that we feel we could not have thought of them until we read about them; yet they too can engender a mood of belief; we accept them into our acquaintance. I think of certain characters in *The Brothers Karamazov*, old Karamazov in particular, characters quite outside our knowledge, and yet real. They are like additions to our experience. Again there are characters which we take on trust with some misgivings, like some of Thackeray's, and Becky Sharp in particular, out of whom certain qualities have been left in order to demonstrate something; and as soon as the imagination tries to demonstrate something outside itself, no matter for what good purpose, it loses some of its truth. Imagination is, indeed, the most imperfect thing; it is not dependable; it can come and go, it is subject to temptations, it can be carried away and lose the balance which Coleridge described. It must always remain imperfect, and the justification for its imperfection is that it gives us a more profound and various understanding of life than personal experience or practical sense ever can. That is its main use, and that is why no humane and civilised society can dispense with it.

This main indispensable use or imagination could be illustrated from the work of any great poet or novelist. But perhaps the poet where we can see it most clearly and visibly at work is Wordsworth, for in him it is involved with things recollected. *The Prelude* is a poem about the imagination and shows it at work. The *Lines composed a few miles above Tintern Abbey* describe the mood in which it was given to him:

> *that blessed mood*
> *In which the burthen of the mystery,*
> *In which the heavy and the weary weight*
> *Of all this unintelligible world*
> *Is lightened:—that serene and blessed mood*
> *In which the affections gently lead us on,—*
> *Until, the breath of this corporeal frame*
> *And even the motion of our human blood*
> *Almost suspended, we are laid asleep*
> *In body, and become a living soul:*
> *While with an eye made quiet by the power*
> *Of harmony, and the deep power of joy,*
> *We see into the life of things.*

What Wordsworth describes is partly a physical, partly a spiritual state, and a vision which only in that state was given to him. Later he lost the vision, as we know, yet he went on writing, for he had a stubborn will. Again and again in *The Prelude* we see the imagination directly working on experience, as we see it in no other poem. We can think of it either as a seeing into the life of things, or if that claim appears excessive, as an uncommon attention concentrated on experiences which for most of us would appear ordinary. He tells how he grew up

> *Fostered alike by beauty and by fear,*

and how guilt sometimes changed the look of things for him. As a boy climbing among the fells, he tells how he was tempted to steal a bird caught in another boy's snare:

> *And, when the deed was done,*
> *I heard among the solitary hills*
> *Low breathings coming after me, and sounds*
> *Of indistinguishable motion, steps*
> *Almost as silent as the turf they trod.*

Shortly afterwards he stole a skiff on the banks of Patterdale one evening. The moon was shining and he pushed off into the lake, gazing at the familiar mountains, when from behind the farthest one

> *a huge Cliff*
> *As if by voluntary power instinct*
> *Upreared its head. I struck and struck again,*
> *And gaining still in stature the grim shape*
> *Towered up between me and the stars, and still,*
> *For so it seemed, with purpose of its own*
> *And measured motion like a living thing,*
> *Strode after me.*

He returned the boat to its place,

> *And through the meadows homeward went, in grave*
> *And serious mood; but after I had seen*

That spectacle, for many days, my brain
Worked with a dim and undetermined sense
Of unknown modes of being; o'er my thoughts
There hung a darkness, call it solitude
Or blank desertion. No familiar shapes
Remained, no pleasant images of trees,
Of sea or sky, no colours of green fields;
But huge and mighty forms, that do not live
Like living men, moved slowly through my mind
By day, and were a trouble to my dreams.

The boy's imagination was wakened by that terrifying experience, and reawakened many years later when Wordsworth was writing *The Prelude*, and realised that he grew up

Fostered alike by beauty and by fear.

Practical intelligence could have told him by then that the huge cliff which pursued him was a childish delusion; but he was not content with that. The experience was real, and he gave it that uncommon attention which is due to real and inexplicable things. He advances no explanation of his terrors that evening, or their effect on his waking life afterwards. He puts them in their place by recalling that as a young boy he

felt the sentiment of Being spread
O'er all that moves, and all that seemeth still. . . .
O'er all that leaps, and runs, and shouts, and sings,
Or beats the gladsome air; o'er all that glides
Beneath the waves, yea, in the wave itself
And mighty depth of water.

And he adds that he conversed then

With things that really are.

I think the greatest poetry in *The Prelude* rises from incidents such as these, rather than from the great generalising passages. They are incidents which to the practical mind would seem ordinary or even trivial, to be explained or explained away. To the imagination they are filled with meaning.

In *The Prelude* we see the imagination working at two stages, first on the incident itself, and then on recollection where it takes on a universal significance. In this way the poem illustrates the source and operation of the imagination. But there is poetry where the imagination is simply present, so that we do not ask from what source it comes, or feel that it is recollected. And in some of his shorter poems Wordsworth displays this kind of imagination too, most powerfully, I think, in *The Affliction of Margaret*—; yet here too we can trace by chance its origin, though its operation has little connection with that. Margaret, we are told, was an old woman who kept a shop in Penrith. Her son had run off to sea and never returned. As a boy Wordsworth had seen her rush out into the street looking wildly about her, hoping that her son had returned at last. That is the source of the poem, and it shows how apparently slight an impression can start the imagination working. The poem describes the varied sequence of feelings that pass through the mind of Margaret:

> *To have despaired, have hoped, believed,*
> *And been forevermore beguiled;*
> *Sometimes with thoughts of very bliss!*
> *I catch at them, and then I miss:*
> *Was ever darkness like to this?*

Her fears for her son grow into a vision of unknown dangerous places of the earth, for she does not know where he may be, and communicate themselves next to ordinary harmless things:

> *My apprehensions come in crowds,*
> *I dread the rustling of the grass;*
> *The very shadows of the clouds*
> *Have power to shake me as they pass.*

She reflects at last that her grief cannot be known by anyone else, though her neighbours feel sorry for her. The odd behaviour of a poor crazed woman is the origin of the poem; the poem itself shows how by means of the imagination her grief can be made present to us.

I would like to turn again to the fact that the dead can move us so deeply when we read about them in a work of imagination, and try to find a more satisfactory explanation for it than divine madness. Hugo von Hofmannsthal said once that great imagination is always conservative. By this he may have meant that it keeps intact the bond which unites us with the past of mankind, so that we can still understand Odysseus and Penelope and the people of the Old Testament. Or he may have meant something more: that imagination is able to do this because it sees the life of everyone as the endless repetition of a universal pattern. It is hard to explain how we can enter into the lives of people long dead, if this is not so. Imagination tells us that we become human by repetition, that our life is a rehearsal of lives that have been lived over and over, and that this act, with all that is good and evil in it, is a theme for delighted and awed contemplation. Or Hofmannsthal may have meant that in the past only is the human pattern complete, that there is the place to which the present turns back to find its finished and timeless pattern. So that the present is a question perpetually running back to find its answer at a place where all is over. The difficulties of the present provoke anger; set in the past they evoke a different emotion. The great public figures who have spread suffering and terror over nations in our time sometimes resolve themselves into actors in a tragedy, or a tragicomedy. We can feel but we cannot see life whole until it has been placed in some kind of past where it discovers its true shape.

We live in a world created by applied science, and our present is unlike the present of any other age. The difference between our world and the world of imagination is growing greater, and may become so great that the one can hardly understand any longer the other. Applied science shows us a world of consistent, mechanical progress. There machines give birth to ever new generations of machines, and the new machines are always better and more efficient than the old, and begin where the old left off. If we could attribute sentience to a new machine, we should find that it simply did not understand the old, being too far ahead, in another world. But in the world of human beings all is different; there we find no mechanical progress, no starting where a previous generation left off; instead there is a continuity ruled by repetition. Every human being has to begin at the beginning, as his forebears did, with the same difficulties and pleasures, the same temptations, the same problem of good and evil, the same inward conflict, the same need to learn how to live, the same inclination to ask what life means. Conspicuous virtue, when this creature encounters it, may move him, or a new and saving faith, since the desire for goodness and truth is also in his nature. Nevertheless he will pass through the same ancestral pattern and have the same feelings, the same difficulties as generations long before he was born. All this may seem dull to the thinker, but it enchants the imagination, for it is an image of human life. But when outward change becomes too rapid, and the world around us alters from year to year, the ancestral image grows indistinct, and the imagination cannot pierce to it as easily as it once could.

Yet at the same time we are bound, even when we do not know it, to the past generations by the same bond that unites us with our neighbours, and if only for the sake of preserving the identity of mankind we must cherish that connection. Fortunately, in spite of our machines, the habits of the human heart remain what they have always been, and imagination deals with them as no other faculty can. It is more urgently needed in our time than ever before.

A VIEW OF POETRY

WE all find it more difficult at present to have a comprehensive view of poetry than people of other times; I mean a view taking in all the various moods and forms of poetry from, let us say, Homer to Dylan Thomas. I do not pretend to offer you this ideally comprehensive view. I should like instead to suggest some conclusions I have come to which help to explain our difficulties in reaching one.

The first thing we must keep in mind is that English poetry is just beginning slowly to recover from a crisis which it had to undergo in the first decades of this century. Roughly forty years ago, for the good of its future, if it was to have one, poetry had to submit to a phase of almost surgical experiment. A crisis of that kind is not a new experience for poetry; it has happened before and it will happen again, for the style of poetry now and then tends to harden until poets can no longer say what they want to say, and new styles have to be found to enable them to speak freely. These periodic crises, in which poetry returns to its self, are really a return to the current language 'spoken by men', to use Wordsworth's phrase, at the time. Dryden, in an age when language was governed by reason, adopted the language of reason and helped to form a new style in poetry. Wordsworth in his turn, when language was governed by feeling, adopted the language of feeling. Both Dryden and Wordsworth, in doing this, followed the imperative mood of their time.

Now, compared with the experiments these two poets made in poetry—Wordsworth makes it clear in the *Lyrical*

Ballads that he was attempting an experiment, he uses the word several times, and Coleridge in his essay on Wordsworth in the *Biographia Literaria* confirms it—compared with these experiments, the modern experiment associated with the names of T. S. Eliot and Ezra Pound, was a very drastic affair. I fancy that the more old-fashioned lovers of Pope, on first reading Wordsworth, would at least have recognised his verses as poetry, if only as bad poetry. But readers of the early Eliot, accustomed to romantic verse, at first did not recognise what they read as poetry at all. I speak from my own experience, but I should add that since then I have acquired a high admiration for Mr. Eliot as a poet. I am merely trying to find a convenient measure for the radical nature of the overturn of poetry in the 'teens and twenties of the century.

I have no doubt of the necessity for that experiment, or of the value of what it did for poetry. But I think it tried to do too much in too short a time, and this had all sorts of unexpected consequences. In returning to common life and common speech, Wordsworth was doing something new in his time, but something that could be understood by the mind and feelings, whether one approved or disapproved of it. But if we take the greatest poem of the modern movement in poetry, *The Waste Land*, we find in it, or rather we found at the time when it appeared, so many new things being done simultaneously, that the result was confused, or what we call in our contemporary vocabulary obscure. I remember when I read it first, soon after it came out, I was partly repelled and partly confounded. I have come since then to admire it greatly; it no longer repels but sympathetically moves me; and I think that this is not an unusual experience among men of my generation: the intellectual and the emotional confusion which the poem generated have been dissolved by repeated readings of it, and by something which one can only call time. For poems of the same kind as *The Waste Land*, though not of the same quality, continued to appear; a movement began, and soon established itself. We can say now that there was one kind of poetry written before Mr. Eliot, and another kind after. He set a convention, as Dryden did and as Wordsworth did, and a convention makes easy what would otherwise remain difficult. If *The Waste Land* had been left as the solitary representative of a new kind of poetry, we should probably still be confused; the critic would still be shaking his half-admiring, half-bewildered head over it. I know that this is a purely fanciful hypothesis, but I advance it merely to point the extraordinary nature of the experiment that was carried out in poetry by Mr. Eliot and some of his contemporaries, and the difference between it and Wordsworth's experiment. The main difference was that it cut far more deeply than Wordsworth did into the substance of poetry, with an analytical knife, and that it attempted far more things without explaining what they were. The result, which I felt was certainly not designed, was a convention of obscurity which lasted through the writing lifetime of the generation that succeeded Mr. Eliot. He himself was sometimes difficult because he was doing something which was difficult; some of his successors were difficult because they thought that poetry should be difficult.

The political poets of the thirties, all of them influenced by Mr. Eliot as poets, and all of them reacting against him as social theorists, seemed to find a temporary solution for poetry, but they found it by the wrong means, for the clarity they achieved as an ideological and not an imaginative clarity. Poets like Dylan Thomas, who reacted in turn against the political poets, fell into a new and deeper obscurity, quite unlike Mr. Eliot's. The latest generation of poets (poetic generations seem to appear and pass with a rapidity in our day which has no parallel in past times) the latest generation seem to be returning to lucidity and form. But the position is still confused; there is no ruling style such as there was among the Augustans and the Romantics; the obscure and the lucid flower side by side, in a sort of reciprocal neglect. All these things which have happened since the revolution started by Mr. Eliot's poetry and criticism cannot hide the value, as I say, of what he did; he did what had to be done, and even those like myself who have not been influenced by him, or are unconscious that they have been, must on purely poetic grounds be thankful to him. Yet when someone does what has to be done, heaven knows what consequences may follow, along with the undeniably salutary ones.

These consequences, it seems to me, are to be found as clearly in criticism as in poetry. I do not mean that they follow from Mr. Eliot's criticism, for he is a critic in the grand traditional style, and I think the greatest critic we have had since Coleridge. It is his poetry, and the poetry of his successors, that has been the innocent occasion of a new kind of criticism which has since established a great influence both over itself (a sort of family influence) and over our ideas of poetry as well. For Mr. Eliot's poetry was admittedly difficult; it had to be read again and again if one were to get to the heart of it, and after that commentated and analysed, or so its more serious critics seemed to think. And from this, criticism went on to conclude that all poetry is difficult, a thing to be enquired into, as if it were a scientific problem. Mr. Eliot made the best reply to that notion himself, when he said that poetry begins and ends in enjoyment.

The New Criticism has many virtues; it is painstaking and conscientious, and it tries to be exact; yet I cannot read it myself without a slight onset of claustrophobia and a feeling that I am being shut in with the critic and the poem, which is generally quite a short one, knowing that I shall not get away until all three of us are exhausted. I have read an essay on Tennyson's *Tears, Idle Tears*, for instance, which goes into a painful analysis of that simple and beautiful poem, enquiring whether the tears were really idle, or if the 'happy autumn fields' would have had a different signification if they had been 'happy April fields'. This is an extreme example of the method. You may say that analysis of this kind has a value in discovering in a poem meanings which an ordinary acquaintance with it might pass without notice; and this is true. Yet there are different ways of knowing a poem; the imaginative way which does not hold up its movement, and the analytical way which arrests it every now and then to examine a line, or even a word, and will not be pried away from that enchanting occupation. Where the analytical critic has imagination, like William Empson, for example, he can discover new sources of delight in a poem. But more often what he discovers, even there, is delight in the fascinating workings of his own mind. And when the analytical critic is without imagination, he is thrown back upon a mere method, a sort of machine through which poems have to be passed in order that they may produce a result which I cannot help feeling that he had in his mind beforehand. This method, in spite of itself, contracts the scope of the poem in a mechanical way, and I have heard that it has influenced the writing of the younger poets, until they are tempted to write poems approved by the method, instead of dictated by themselves. If that is true, then it is a disaster; but I cannot believe it to be true.

The animating spirit of poetry is imagination, and the work of the imagination is to seize life as it lives and moves, in its individuality, just as it is the work of the analytical intellect to arrest it in order to discover the elements out of which it is made or the laws by which it works. The analytical intellect, especially in the sciences, has had a marvellous development in the last two hundred years; the greatest powers of mankind in the western world have gone into it, and not into imagination and poetry. Leopardi, more than a hundred years ago, speaking of the melancholy of his contemporaries, attributed it to the withering of the imagination, caused by the loss of a world explainable by myth, that is a world imaged in its individuality, as it lived and moved, and he felt that nature was no longer animate and sentient but mechanical and necessary. Wordsworth said that in the moment of poetic imagination we see into the life of things. But what life remains in things when they have become mechanical? I think that Leopardi said something of extraordinary penetration in speaking of a nature which had become mechanical, but something, nevertheless, only half-true. Things still have their unique and individual life, as they have had from the start; that life has only become more difficult to reach through a thickening maze of abstractions and the secondary mechanical world we have manufactured out of the world by the immense ingenuity of applied science. This may be one of the main reasons why it is more difficult to write poetry now than it was in the past; and one of the causes of the uncertainty and obscurity of poetry. But the nature of poetry has not changed, and in our own time has resurrected, for instance, the myths which Leopardi thought were gone for ever; they have been brought back in order that the imagination might see farther into the life of things, and past the flat image which the life of the contemporary world gives us. The contemporary image cannot be ignored; the modern world is important to us simply because it is the world in which we live; but it takes on a deeper significance when we see it as rooted in a past whose extent we cannot measure, and perhaps never will be able to measure. Imagination unites us with humanity in time and space; by means of it we understand Hector and Achilles in their distant world, and feel the remote emotion in a Chinese poem; in such things we are at one with universal mankind and with ourselves. That is the work of the imagination, and our lives would not have any meaning if they were quite without it. So that to treat poetry scientifically, to analyse a poem as if it were a curious object, or simply a problem, and not a mysterious mode of apprehension natural and necessary to mankind, is to approach it from the blind side. Gabriel Marcel makes an illuminating distinction between the problem and the mystery: the problem is somewhere outside us, it is there to be solved and we are the solvers; the mystery is within us; we are the main factor: we can never solve ourselves; we are involved. Poetry puts us in this relation, and perhaps it is our realisation of this that makes us feel, after no matter how brilliant an analysis of a poem, that it is not enough, and that it is not even relevant. Besides, the strain of standing outside a poem while this prolonged scrutiny is carried on is an unnatural strain. This is not what poetry was made for, not what Shakespeare or any poet intended in the moment of poetic creation.

Poetry has contracted in the last hundred and particularly in the last fifty years; it has become more and more conscious of itself, and less and less aware of its audience, while its audience grows smaller and smaller. Yet at the same time knowledge about our life on the earth has greatly increased; psychology, anthropology, archaeology and other sciences have produced a great mass of new material on which the imagination can work. The myth has been resurrected; buried thoughts, buried modes of existence have been brought into the light: so that poetry has potentially a far greater, and I think a far more exciting province to deal with than it had in Wordsworth's time. Something has been done already, and I feel that we are not at the end of poetry, as some appear to think, but perhaps, without knowing it, on the verge of a new beginning. A beginning can sometimes be more despairing than an ending; poetic modes die peacefully; the romantic movement painlessly dreamed itself out in the dream poetry of William Morris. We know, on the other hand, how hard were the birth pangs of modern poetry. The difficulty of the poet now is that the possible world of imagination lying before him has grown unmanageably; he does not know where to attack it; it seems beyond expression. He is distracted by having too much before him. At the same time he is daunted by the danger of our age. Gabriel Marcel says we live in a time in which it is possible at last for mankind to commit suicide. I do not believe in that possibility, nor that poetry itself can commit suicide. We have before us the possibility of a poetry greater in its resources than was ever envisaged before; we have on the other hand a tendency to contract the poem to a schematic pattern. Perhaps the contraction is a prudential safeguard against the rush of an almost lawless expansion. But a measure will be reached in time, when we have overcome the excesses of prudence, and the imagination may yet work within its own free bounds again.

INDEX

INDEX

PRINTED IN GREAT BRITAIN
BY R. & R. CLARK, LTD., EDINBURGH